Arma Christi

or

The Weapons of Our Warfare

Daily Meditations for Lent
on
the Instruments of the Passion

by the
Carmelites of the Holy Face

Lovingly dedicated to Our Lord Jesus Christ the King, who left us the instruments of His Passion as tokens of His great victory over sin and death and as weapons to aid us in the spiritual combat. May the following pages help fellow soldiers of Christ to skilfully employ these weapons, and thus hasten the defeat of "revolutionary men."

carmelitesholyface.com

All quotations from Holy Scripture are taken from the Douay-Rheims Bible.

ISBN: 9781805173373

In obedience to the decrees of Pope Urban VIII, we declare that we have no intention of attributing any other than a purely human authority to the miracles, revelations, favours, and sanctity of uncanonised persons referred to in this book.

We declare, moreover, that we submit with all our hearts to the unchanging Magisterium of the Holy Roman Catholic Church. If there is in this book anything contrary to Her teaching, it is not intentional and we willingly retract it. Given the current Crisis in the Church, which has made it impossible to obtain an imprimatur by going through the usual channels, it has been deemed sufficient to have these pages reviewed by a competent bishop, who is faithful to Holy Tradition.

"For though we walk in the flesh, we do not war according to the flesh. For the weapons of our warfare are not carnal, but mighty to God unto the pulling down of fortifications, destroying counsels, and every height that exalteth itself against the knowledge of God; and bringing into captivity every understanding unto the obedience of Christ; and having in readiness to revenge all disobedience, when your obedience shall be fulfilled."

2 Corinthians 10:3-6

Contents

Introduction

The Arma Christi (Instruments of the Passion or Weapons of Christ) are the objects associated with the Passion of Our Lord, His suffering, death, and burial. In medieval times there was a great devotion to the Arma Christi. Illustrated manuscripts from as early as the ninth century make reference to the different instruments of the Passion, often in the form of a poem accompanied by appropriate drawings.[1] In the ages of chivalry, various instruments of the Passion featured on the coat of arms belonging to certain devout families. They were not infrequently incorporated in stone engravings on tombs and high crosses throughout Ireland and England.

The Arma Christi were also depicted in a variety of paintings, especially dating from the fourteenth and fifteenth centuries. There doesn't appear to be any fixed number of these instruments. Other symbols have also been incorporated by artists which cannot, strictly speaking, be considered as instruments, but which do inspire deeper reflection on the Passion. The pelican feeding its young with its blood is one such symbol. The bloody footprints of Christ are another. In this collection of meditations, we have endeavoured to include only those objects which were directly associated with Christ's Passion. Not all of these are mentioned in the Gospel, but nearly all find their place in the traditional depictions of the Arma Christi. Doubtless there are others we have not included, but those which are found herein are sufficient to provide daily meditations for Lent. Of course they may be used at other times as well, even outside this holy season.

[1] See the appendix for a translation of one of these medieval poems.

In the eighteenth century, at the request of the Passionist Order, Pope Pius VI approved of Offices and Masses for several feasts in honour of certain instruments of the Passion. Some of these feasts had already been requested by and celebrated in particular dioceses, even from as early as the thirteenth century. These feasts are assigned to the various Fridays during Lent and can sometimes be found in an appendix to the Roman Missal. The instruments thus officially venerated are included in this book on the day corresponding to their respective feast. There is one exception: the Feast of the Holy Lance and Nails is kept on the same day, but we have assigned the meditation on the nails to a different day. When instituting this feast for Germany and Bohemia in 1353, Pope Innocent VI said: *"We should honour the most holy Passion of our Lord and Redeemer, Jesus Christ, in such manner that, meditating on all the mysteries and merits of the same Passion, we venerate also each sacred instrument thereof."*

The Arma Christi are also associated with several Marian images and apparitions. The ancient icon of Our Lady of Perpetual Succour includes two angels holding instruments of the Passion: the cross, the reed, and the lance. When Our Lady appeared at La Salette in 1846, she had two instruments of the Passion, the hammer, and pliers (symbolic of reparation) attached to the crucifix she was wearing. In 1878 she appeared to Marie-Julie Jahenny, asking her to have a purple scapular made. This purple scapular also contains a number of the instruments of the Passion. Our Lady explained the meaning of the image on the front of this scapular: *"The nails that have pierced the feet and the hands of my Son have been little venerated and are venerable, hence my Son, in His Divine Wisdom, has made that these three nails be painted on the front of the scapular. These three drops of blood and the chalice represent the generous hearts gathering the Blood of my Divine Son. The red sponge will represent my Divine Son drinking, in a manner, the sins of His children but His Adorable Mouth refuses."*

Our Lord explained the meaning of the back image: *"My children, very few souls think of wiping the Adorable Wounds of My Feet when the Blood ran and I would like this representation to be known. They also think so little of the tears shed by My Mother during My Passion; these tears are found at the feet of the Angel that wipes My Sacred Feet. By this scapular, I would like you to think on the ladder, the reed and the nails of My Passion."*[2]

It is a great pity that the devotion to the Arma Christi has fallen into decline; and, in view of the apparitions and revelations mentioned above, it is clearly the will of God that it should be revived. The increased devotion to the Holy Face of Jesus in recent times also leads us to hope that this medieval devotion will receive more attention, for the two are closely connected with one another, and both have been indicated as being the divine remedy for Communism. They are also intimately linked with the work of reparation. When God's love for mankind has been neglected by forgetfulness or violated by offence, some sort of compensation must be rendered for the injury, and this debt is commonly called by the name of reparation. The need for reparation is surely evident to men and women of faith.

We are in the midst of the greatest battle in history. It is a battle all the greater in that it is a spiritual one. Communism adopts many different names and disguises, but it gives itself away by its erroneous philosophy which is in stark contrast to Christianity. It is not merely a battle for land or for temporal power. It is not merely a struggle to unite the nations in a new world order where each one is at liberty to believe what they

[2] Vision and revelation of 23 August, 1878

choose and to act as they please. Essentially it is a battle for the souls of mankind. The communists are but instruments in the hands of Satan who is using them to make war on the Church and to drag souls to Hell. To effectively combat them, we must arm ourselves with divine weapons.

In 1847, after warning her of the approaching threat of Communism, Our Lord said to Sr. Mary of St. Peter: *"To arm you for the battle ahead, I give you the weapons of My Passion, that is My Cross which these enemies dread, and also the other instruments of My tortures."*[3] From this it is clear that it is not only the Holy Face Devotion, but also the Arma Christi which Heaven has indicated as being our means of defeating the *"revolutionary men."*

The Venerable Léon Dupont was also well aware of the need for supernatural weapons. He used to say: *"Since we cannot descend into Hell to chain up Satan there, let us go to the Heart of Jesus in search of the weapons wherewith to combat him on earth."*[4] In the Heart of Jesus we shall surely find the instruments of His Passion which are the divine weapons He wills us to employ. They are symbolic of the various kinds of sufferings He endured for our salvation. Each of these sufferings was offered in expiation for a particular kind of sin. In that sense, each instrument associated in the reparation for that sin is also symbolic of the contrary virtue.

To the souls whom Our Lord loves most, and to those who love Him best, He generally grants a deeper share in His sufferings and a greater participation in His Passion than most Christians experience. Veronica Giuliani was one such soul. She was

---

[3] "The Golden Arrow," (TAN Books, North Carolina, 2012) p.203; revelation of 29 March, 1847

[4] "The Life of Léon Papin-Dupont", by Edward Healy Thompson, based on the work of Abbe Janvier, Ch. 14

an Italian Capuchin nun who was remarkable for her spirit of penance, and who received the stigmata. So deeply had she entered into and participated in the sufferings of Christ, that when her heart was opened after her death, in 1727, it was found to contain a variety of instruments of the Passion. Such souls are rare, however; and most Christians consider the instruments of the sufferings of Our Lord as nothing more than precious relics of the past.

Among the faithful there is a growing awareness of the need for a divine remedy to counteract the spread of atheistic communism. At present, however, while praiseworthy attention is given to the Holy Face Devotion, the importance and relevance of the Arma Christi is generally overlooked. It is true that they are mentioned in one of the prayers of the Holy Face chaplet,[5] but beyond that, devout people are often at a loss to know how to make further use of these weapons, and so they are neglected.

There are many reasons why these are most appropriate weapons for the battle against the Communists and revolutionary men who continue the revolt of Lucifer and echo his *"Non serviam—I will not serve."* One of the fundamental errors of Communism is that it seeks to establish a material paradise here on earth, independently of God. It is an illusion to think that this is possible. Sin and death cannot be conquered except through the merits of the Passion of Our Lord Jesus Christ. Perfect happiness cannot be attained except through suffering, and Christians must suffer with Christ if they are to gain the heavenly crown. The Arma Christi are visible reminders of these truths. By means of the pain these instruments inflicted

[5] "Eternal Father, I offer Thee the cross of Our Lord Jesus Christ, and all the other instruments of His Holy Passion, that Thou mayest put division in the camp of Thy enemies, for as Thy Beloved Son has said, a kingdom divided against itself shall fall."

on Our Lord, the world was redeemed and Satan was vanquished. They are the weapons by which His great victory was won.

The effects of this victory, however, are impeded by the passions, evil tendencies and self-seeking of man's lower nature. Christ has redeemed us, but He has not taken away our free will or our ability to commit sin, which is an abuse of free will. The life of every good Christian is a renewal of the life of Christ and His battle against sin. Through Him, with Him and in Him, we are certain of the victory. We cannot conquer alone. It is a struggle to keep our lower nature in check and to live in obedience to God and His will, but in the Arma Christi we have a visible reminder of the victory in store for those who persevere in fighting the good fight. Even as they have become precious trophies of His triumph, so also will our sufferings add to the glory of our heavenly crown if we accept them in a Christian spirit.

By meditating on the sufferings of Our Lord in His Passion, we realise something of the hideousness and gravity of sin. The instruments of the Passion are powerful visual aids to help us call to mind the various scenes with which they are connected. They bring home to us the depths of God's love for mankind which led Him to endure so much for our salvation. At the sight of such love, what other response can we make than to see to it that His Blood has not been shed for us in vain? In practice this means taking every precaution to avoid sin ourselves, and also endeavouring to obtain for sinners the grace of repentance. This necessarily involves self-denial, and human nature instinctively shrinks from pain; but the bitterness of mortification is greatly lessened when it is united to the sufferings of Christ.

As we reflect on each instrument in turn, love will suggest little ways in which we can make an appropriate use of it, uniting some small mortification of our own to the suffering it inflicted on Jesus. For example, if we are meditating on the blindfold, we can refrain from looking at something pleasant while thinking of how Our Lord was mortified in His sense of sight. This could be offered as an act of reparation for those who indulge the sense of sight too freely and also for our own sins in that regard.

It is in the hope of reviving the medieval devotion to the Arma Christi that the following meditations are being made available to the public. They were composed some years ago and were originally intended to be merely a devotional exercise for within our own Community during Lent. Since then they have been expanded and developed, with an original painting for each one. The Scripture references provided are merely a guide to stimulate deeper reflection on the relevant instrument and are not exhaustive. The poem and brief meditation accompanying each instrument suggests how it can be used to make appropriate reparation for a particular kind of sin, and hints at the need to examine our own conscience in that regard. The prayers are sufficiently brief to enable them to be memorised or copied out and used as ejaculations throughout the day. They, too, are merely a guide, intended to help you maintain your focus on the Passion and to employ the instrument of the day in the spiritual combat. They are by no means intended to prevent you from composing your own.

Let us earnestly invoke Our Lady's help in this battle, while following her example of fidelity to grace, and we may be confident of success. To Mary we may apply the words of the inspired writer, whom the Church invokes as the Tower of David: *"Thy neck, is as the tower of David, which is built with bulwarks: a thousand bucklers hang upon it, all the armour of valiant men.*"[6] May the Blessed Virgin Mary, the Royal Treasury of God and the Mediatrix of His graces to mankind, teach us how to use these weapons wisely and help us to persevere in the fight until we come to share in the glory of the eternal victory!

[6] Canticle of Canticles 4:4

Dear Christian soul, draw near to Christ
As you this Lent begin;
Recall the way He paid the price
To ransom you from sin.

The weapons of His victory
Must be your armour too,
So ponder on the mystery
Of each this whole Lent through.

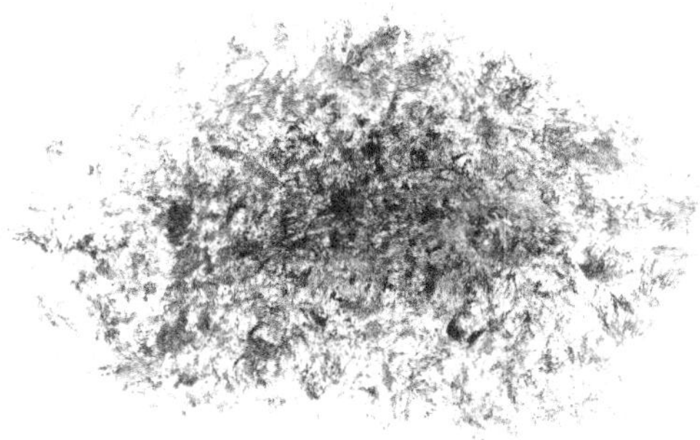

Ash Wednesday

Dust

Remember, man, that dust thou art;
To dust thou shalt return.
Lay up this lesson in thy heart,
And earthly glory spurn.

Remember Jesus Crucified,
A Worm, despised by men;
Atone today for sins of pride,
For which He suffered then.

"In the sweat of thy face shalt thou eat bread till thou return to the earth, out of which thou wast taken: for dust thou art, and into dust thou shalt return."

—Genesis 3:19

"And Abraham answered, and said: Seeing I have once begun, I will speak to my Lord, whereas I am dust and ashes."

—Genesis 18:27

"Let the enemy pursue my soul, and take it, and tread down my life on the earth, and bring down my glory to the dust."

—Psalm 7:6

"But I am a worm, and no man: the reproach of men, and the outcast of the people…My strength is dried up like a potsherd, and my tongue hath cleaved to my jaws: and thou hast brought me down into the dust of death."

—Psalm 21:7,16

"As a father hath compassion on his children, so hath the Lord compassion on them that fear him: For he knoweth our frame. He remembereth that we are dust."

—Psalm 102:14

Meditation

The penitential season of Lent very fittingly begins with a lesson in humility. As the priest marks the faithful with blessed ashes, he reminds them of the fact that we are dust. This is the same admonition Adam received after he had sinned. To sin is to exalt oneself and refuse to submit to the will of God, preferring to follow one's own will. That is pride – the very opposite of humility. In the Passion, Our Lord left us a model of humility. No creature has ever abased itself so greatly, though none was so worthy of veneration. Although the Sacred Body of Jesus, being free from all sin, was exempt from the law of nature by which man returns to dust, He suffered all the torments of being reduced to dust and treated as a sinner during His Passion. Like *a worm and no man*, He was trampled upon and despised as the most abject and worthless of creatures. When Jesus fell on His way to Calvary, the dust clung to His bleeding wounds, especially those of His most Holy Face, and increased His sufferings. He Who is the Lamb without blemish, suffered this torment; taking upon Himself our iniquities so that we might be made clean.

Let us make special reparation today for sins of pride by which man, who is dust, prefers himself to God; and also for those who live without a thought for their final destiny. We can do this by considering ourselves as God's servants, attentively seeking His will and faithfully carrying it out.

Prayers

Eternal Father, I offer Thee all the humiliations which Jesus suffered in His Sacred Passion, particularly in being trampled upon in the dust, in reparation for sins of pride and for those who do not consider their final destiny.

Lord Jesus Christ, have mercy on us sinners, who are no better than dust and ashes. Help us to rise to a more perfect life through the humble penance we undertake this Lent.

Thursday After Ash Wednesday

Horn/Trumpet

The mob had their attention drawn
To Jesus, whom they mocked.
When hearing this resounding horn,
Around the Lord they flocked.

On Judgement Day the horn shall sound;
O Christian soul, prepare!
Again shall all be gathered round,
But woe to mockers there.

"And forthwith he sounded the trumpet in mount Ephraim: and the children of Israel went down with him, he himself going in the front."

—Judges 3:27

"God is ascended with jubilee, and the Lord with the sound of trumpet."

—Psalm 46:6

"Praise Him with sound of trumpet: praise Him with psaltery and harp."

—Psalm 150:3

"All ye inhabitants of the world, who dwell on the earth, when the sign shall be lifted up on the mountains, you shall see, and you shall hear the sound of the trumpet."

—Isaias 18:3

"And it shall come to pass, that in that day a noise shall be made with a great trumpet, and they that were lost, shall come from the land of the Assyrians, and they that were outcasts in the land of Egypt, and they shall adore the Lord in the holy mount in Jerusalem."

—Isaias 27:13

"Blow ye the trumpet in Sion, sound an alarm in My holy mountain, let all the inhabitants of the land tremble: because the day of the Lord cometh, because it is nigh at hand."

—Joel 2:1

"And he shall send his angels with a trumpet, and a great voice: and they shall gather together his elect from the four winds, from the farthest parts of the heavens to the utmost bounds of them."

—Matthew 24:31

Meditation

The trumpet or horn was customarily used to draw the attention of the public to the criminals being led out to death. Prompted by the Scribes and Pharisees, the soldiers did everything they could to increase the humiliation of our Saviour, and we can be sure that they would not have omitted using this instrument, although it is not specifically recorded in the Gospel. Such was the way in which the Jews treated their King. The instruments which should have been used to honour Him were used instead to make a mockery of Christ the King. Even today many people continue to mock our Lord and all that is sacred.

Let us make reparation today for those who create and those who willingly listen to bad music in which the Holy Name of God is often blasphemed and by which the instruments given to mankind for praising God are used instead to perform the work of Satan. This is especially the case with rock and heavy metal music and the majority of profane songs which are so popular in these modern times. We can atone for this by refraining from listening to something lawful and pleasant; also by using our voices and musical abilities to glorify God and sing His praises. By keeping our will harmony with the will of God, we shall offer Him a sacrifice of praise and keep a continual melody in our hearts which will console Him for those who do not.

Prayers

Eternal Father, I offer Thee the humiliation of Jesus in being led before the crowds as a mock king, in reparation for those who dishonour Thee through bad music.

Praised be Jesus Christ, our Lord and our King!

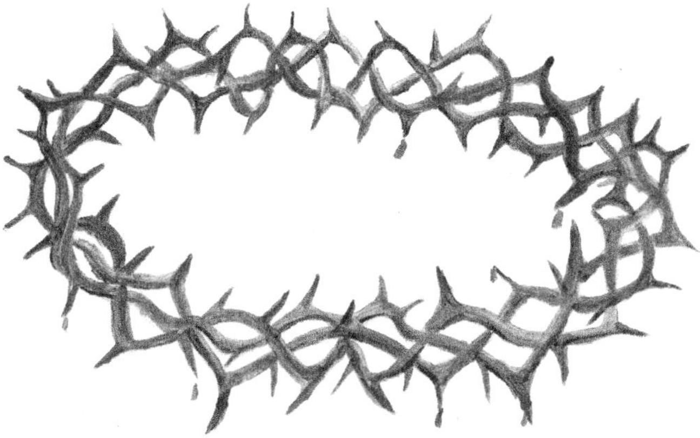

Friday After Ash Wednesday

Feast of the Crown of Thorns

Do you desire true renown?
Then suffer with your God;
Remove the painful thorny crown;
Avert the striking rod.

Console the Church for all the woes
She meets with in Her head;
Atone today for sins of those
By whom souls are misled.

"And to Adam he said: Because thou hast hearkened to the voice of thy wife, and hast eaten of the tree, whereof I commanded thee that thou shouldst not eat, cursed is the earth in thy work; with labour and toil shalt thou eat thereof all the days of thy life. Thorns and thistles shall it bring forth to thee; and thou shalt eat the herbs of the earth."

—Genesis 3:17-18

"For day and night Thy hand was heavy upon me: I am turned in My anguish, whilst the thorn is fastened."

—Psalm 31:4

"For what shall I strike you any more, you that increase transgression? the whole head is sick, and the whole heart is sad. From the sole of the foot unto the top of the head, there is no soundness therein: wounds and bruises and swelling sores: they are not bound up, nor dressed, nor fomented with oil."

—Isaias 1:5-6

"As the lily among thorns, so is my love among the daughters."

—Canticle of Canticles 2:2

"And the soldiers led Him away into the court of the palace, and they called together the whole band: And they clothed Him with purple, and platting a crown of thorns, they put it upon Him."

—Mark 15:16-17

"And the soldiers platting a crown of thorns, put it upon His head; and they put on Him a purple garment."

—John 19:2

Meditation

As a part of Adam's punishment, God decreed that the earth would bring forth thorns and thistles. Thorns are symbolic of sin. The sinless Lamb of God suffered for our sins by wearing a crown of thorns upon His Sacred Head. The Church, like Her Divine Lord and Master, is currently undergoing Her Passion; and once again it is in Her head that She is suffering most. It is the clergy, the hierarchy of the Catholic Church, who have inflicted the most painful wounds upon Her. By apostasy, heresy, schism and compromise they have caused tremendous suffering to the Mystical Body of Christ. Nevertheless, we must not neglect to see the sufferings inflicted on Our Lord by the crown of thorns as the effect of our own sins, especially those of vain ambition, self-esteem, and pride, in all of its forms. We, too, have added to the sufferings of His Mystical Body.

Let us make reparation today for the sins of the clergy and likewise atone for our own sins of pride. We can do this by humbly seeking to perform small and hidden services for others, uniting our efforts to the merits gained by our suffering Saviour through the crown of thorns. In this way we shall remove the thorns from His Head and console Him for the wounds they have inflicted on Him.

Prayers

Eternal Father, I offer Thee all the sufferings of Jesus in wearing the crown of thorns, in reparation for the sins of the clergy and for my own sins of pride.

By the sufferings of Thy thorn-crowned Head, O Jesus, have pity on the clergy and teach me to be truly humble.

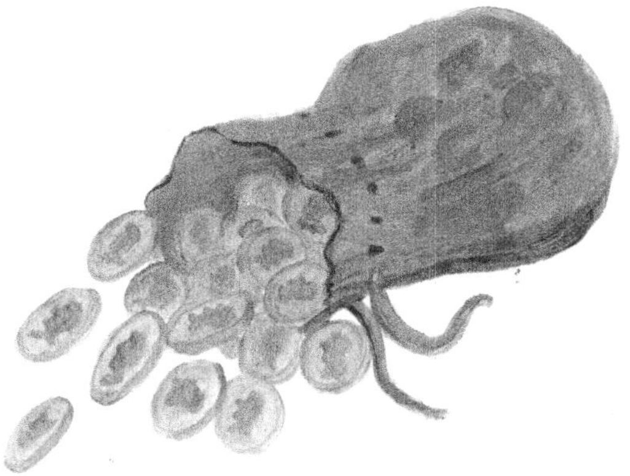

Saturday After Ash Wednesday

Thirty Pieces of Silver

Recall how men prefer to Christ
A fleeting paltry sum;
By avarice and greed enticed,
Like Judas they become.

Atone for those who forfeit grace,
Whose souls are almost lost.
The precious coin of Christ's Own Face
Shall help you pay the cost.

"And when the Madianite merchants passed by, they drew him [Joseph] out of the pit, and sold him to the Ismaelites, for twenty pieces of silver: and they led him into Egypt."

—Genesis 37:28

"And I said to them: If it be good in your eyes, bring hither my wages: and if not, be quiet. And they weighed for my wages thirty pieces of silver. And the Lord said to me: Cast it to the statuary, a handsome price, that I was prized at by them. And I took the thirty pieces of silver, and I cast them into the house of the Lord to the statuary."

—Zacharias 11:12-13

"And he said to them: What will you give me, if I will deliver him unto you? But they appointed him thirty pieces of silver."

—Matthew 26:15

"Then Judas, who betrayed him, seeing that he was condemned, repenting himself, brought back the thirty pieces of silver to the chief priests and ancients Saying: I have sinned in betraying innocent blood. But they said: What is that to us? look thou to it. And casting down the pieces of silver in the temple, he departed: and went and hanged himself with an halter."

—Matthew 27:3-6

Meditation

Behold today how many souls have become like Judas! Many indeed are the poor unfortunate souls who have betrayed their Master, deadened their conscience, lost the garment of grace and exchanged the faith for the temporary pleasures of wealth, power, honour and fame. Yet happiness evades them, for the sinner knows no peace; and a guilty conscience prevents such transitory things from satisfying those who seek them. Oh how miserable are they who turn away from God, who alone can fill the soul to satisfaction with true love, peace and joy! Many are the miserable individuals who have taken their own lives in a vain endeavour to escape from such an unhappy existence. If only those who are now burning with Judas in Hell had repented and had invoked the infinite mercy of God! Let us pray especially today for those who are in despair and those on the point of committing suicide so that even at the last moment they may receive the grace to repent and beg for God's forgiveness. Let us also make reparation for sins of theft, avarice and greed which lead many to follow the example of Judas.

On 28 October 1845 as Sr. Mary of St. Peter was reflecting on the crime of Judas, Our Lord said to her: "in the Kingdom of Heaven you shall obtain all you desire by offering the coin of My precious Humanity which is My Holy Face."[7]

The following ejaculation is easily memorised and will help us to use this precious coin to purchase as many souls as we can. Let us have confidence that our petitions will be granted by means of this offering, for Our Lord has said: "According to your faith, be it done unto you."[8]

---

[7] "The Golden Arrow," p.161

[8] Matthew 9:29

Prayer

Eternal Father, I offer Thee the Holy Face of Jesus as a most precious coin to purchase souls.

First Sunday in Lent

Washbowl and Pitcher

The jug and basin have displayed
What history can't efface:
The guilt incurred by one afraid
To justly judge the case.

Let's stand by Truth which men reject,
Courageous; unafraid;
To make amends for false respect
And judgements wrongly made.

"I will wash my hands among the innocent; and will compass thy altar, O Lord."

—Psalm 25:6

"Every one therefore that shall confess me before men, I will also confess him before my Father who is in heaven. But he that shall deny me before men, I will also deny him before my Father who is in heaven."

—Matthew 10:32-33

"And Pilate seeing that he prevailed nothing, but that rather a tumult was made; taking water washed his hands before the people, saying: I am innocent of the blood of this just man; look you to it."

—Matthew 27:24

"But Peter and the apostles answering, said: We ought to obey God, rather than men."

—Acts 5:29

"If we suffer, we shall also reign with Him. If we deny Him, He will also deny us."

—2 Timothy 2:12

Meditation

Pontius Pilate shall always be remembered as the coward who condemned the innocent Jesus to death; a scene which is recalled by the jug and basin which he used in a vain attempt to free himself from guilt. The jug and basin also call to mind how Our Lord washed the feet of His disciples on the night of the Last Supper. This was symbolic of the Sacrament of Penance by which sins are washed away from those who are rightly disposed; that is, those who are truly repentant and intend to amend their lives. Only God has the power to forgive sins, as the Jews rightly claimed; but this power is exercised in His Name by Catholic priests, who are His visible representatives here on earth. Human power alone is incapable of granting the remission of sins. Pontius Pilate's attempt to free himself from guilt was therefore of no avail for the cleansing of his conscience. It is an illusion to make excuses in order to justify oneself while doing something morally wrong, or to think that by pleasing the crowd at the cost of truth and justice one can be exempt from sin.

With these thoughts in mind, let us atone for the sins of all judges who have so great a responsibility to defend the cause of truth and justice; and also for those guilty of making rash judgements. We can do this by making a special endeavour to overcome our human respect, for it is human respect which has caused so many to share in Pilate's cowardice by preferring to offend God rather than displease men. An efficacious way of overcoming this tendency is to begin the day with a pure intention of pleasing God in all that we do, and to renew this intention as often as possible throughout the course of the day.

Prayers

Eternal Father, I offer Thee all my prayers, joys, works and sufferings of this day in reparation for sins of rash judgement and human respect. Help me to keep a pure intention of pleasing Thee in all that I do.

By Thy Precious Blood O Jesus, and by the sorrowful tears of Mary, may our sins be washed away.

Monday First Week in Lent

Blindfold–Sense of Sight

The blindfold which was used to bind
The eyes of Christ that night,
Reproaches all the wilful blind;
Recalls the sense of sight.

For evil men who scandalise
The innocent and small
Let us atone, and guard our eyes
Lest we ourselves should fall.

"And I have given thee for a covenant of the people, for a light of the Gentiles: That thou mightest open the eyes of the blind, and bring forth the prisoner out of prison, and them that sit in darkness out of the prison house."

—Isaias 42:6-7

"And whosoever shall scandalize one of these little ones that believe in me; it were better for him that a millstone were hanged around his neck, and he were cast into the sea."

—Mark 9:41

"And they blindfolded him, and smote his face. And they asked him, saying: Prophesy, who is it that struck thee?"

—Luke 22:64

"He hath blinded their eyes, and hardened their heart, that they should not see with their eyes, nor understand with their heart, and be converted, and I should heal them."

—John 12:40

"In whom the god of this world hath blinded the minds of unbelievers, that the light of the gospel of the glory of Christ, who is the image of God, should not shine unto them."

—2 Corinthians 4:4

"This then I say and testify in the Lord: That henceforward you walk not as also the Gentiles walk in the vanity of their mind, having their understanding darkened, being alienated from the life of God through the ignorance that is in them, because of the blindness of their hearts."

—Ephesians 4:17-18

Meditation

The servants of the high priests covered the eyes of Jesus with a blindfold because they could not bear to meet His gaze. The Truth would have made them see the iniquity of their own hearts and so they preferred to avoid seeing themselves in the light of His Countenance. It is not only the Jews who were guilty of this blindness. We share in this blindness (which is the result of pride) whenever we are unwilling to look deeper into our hearts to discover our failings or refuse to acknowledge the truth that we are sinners.

By the suffering which He endured in having His eyes bound, Jesus atoned for the wilful blind, and also for all sins of sight. Many indeed are those who misuse the sense of sight and those who scandalise little ones through this sense by means of bad movies, indecent pictures and immodest dress. Let us make a special endeavour today to observe custody of the eyes, restraining even our legitimate curiosity, in reparation for these sins. We shall find it helpful to recall the blindfolded Face of Jesus and to offer our mortification of the eyes to the Eternal Father in union with the sufferings endured by His Divine Son in the sense of sight.

Prayers

Eternal Father, I offer Thee the blindfolded Face of Jesus in reparation for the sins of sight and especially for the sins of those who scandalise Thy little ones.

O Lord, may the light of Thy Face shine upon those who are in darkness and enlighten the eyes of the blind.

Lord, that I may see the light!

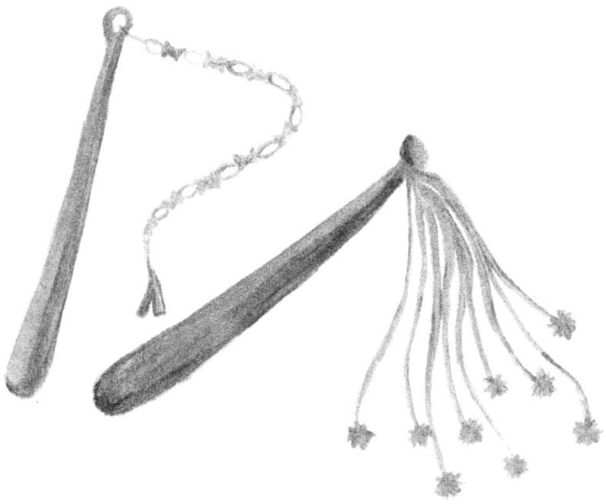

Tuesday First Week in Lent

Scourges—Sense of Touch

To expiate all sins of touch,
The scourges ripped and tore:
Christ's Body suffered very much
Because of the impure.

The Church is suffering as back then,
Made like a den of thieves;
Through penance wield the whip again
Till every traitor leaves.

"For I am ready for scourges: and my sorrow is continually before me."

—Psalm 37:18

"And I have been scourged all the day; and my chastisement hath been in the mornings."

—Psalm 72:14

"If he scourge, let him kill at once, and not laugh at the pains of the innocent."

—Job 9:23

"And so Pilate being willing to satisfy the people, released to them Barabbas, and delivered up Jesus, when he had scourged him, to be crucified."

—Mark 15:15

"For he shall be delivered to the Gentiles, and shall be mocked, and scourged, and spit upon."

—Luke 18:32

"And when he had made, as it were, a scourge of little cords, he drove them all out of the temple, the sheep also and the oxen, and the money of the changers he poured out, and the tables he overthrew."

—John 2:15

"Then therefore, Pilate took Jesus, and scourged him."

—John 19:1

Meditation

Human nature being what it is, mortification has always been needful to keep the flesh in subjection to the spirit. In an age when material comforts abound, mortification is especially necessary. Unless we use the good things of this world in moderation, we risk becoming enslaved to our passions and losing the dignity of children of God. By denying ourselves some of the lawful pleasures which are offered to us, we will be better able to arrive at that detachment which is a needful preparation for union with God. At the same time, if we unite them to the sufferings of Our Lord in His Passion, these acts of self-denial will help to obtain mercy and grace for others.

By the cruel scourging, Our Lord suffered greatly in His sense of touch. The scourges remind us of the immense suffering which this caused Him, not only the physical pain of being scourged, but also the mockery which was made of His most chaste body. Jesus thereby made reparation for sins of impurity, lust, adultery, self-indulgence, and all sins of the flesh.

The scourges also remind us of how Our Divine Lord Himself used a scourge to drive out the money-changers from the temple. Even to this very day, many people continue to make God's house a den of thieves, by stealing from God the honour and respect which is due to Him. By His scourging therefore, Our Lord also atoned for irreverence in the House of God, and for all sins which defile our bodies which are the temples of the Living God. Let us join our Divine Redeemer in making reparation for these sins by offering up our voluntary mortifications in union with His painful scourging.

Prayers

Eternal Father, I offer Thee the painful scourging of Jesus in reparation for the irreverence in Thy Churches and for all sins of impurity.

By Thy painful scourging, O Jesus, may the Church of darkness be driven from Rome.

Wednesday First Week in Lent

Vinegar—Sense of Taste

As on the cross He hung, half-dead,
"I thirst!" the Saviour cried.
They gave Him vinegar instead,
Of that for which He sighed.

It was the love of men He craved
Which many still deny Him;
He thirsted that you might be saved,
Will you not satisfy Him?

"And they gave me gall for my food, and in my thirst they gave me vinegar to drink."

—Psalm 68:22

"And immediately one of them running took a sponge, and filled it with vinegar; and put it on a reed, and gave him to drink."

—Matthew 27:48

"And one running and filling a sponge with vinegar, and putting it upon a reed, gave him to drink, saying: Stay, let us see if Elias come to take him down."

—Mark 15:36

"And the soldiers also mocked him, coming to him, and offering him vinegar."

—Luke 23:36

"Afterwards, Jesus knowing that all things were now accomplished, that the scripture might be fulfilled, said: I thirst. Now there was a vessel set there full of vinegar. And they, putting a sponge full of vinegar and hyssop, put it to his mouth. Jesus therefore, when he had taken the vinegar, said: It is consummated. And bowing his head, he gave up the ghost."

—John 19:28-30

Meditation

How great was the torment of thirst, which our Saviour endured silently until death was near! He had shed torrents of blood during the agony, the scourging, the crowning with thorns and the crucifixion; and not having had anything to drink since the Last Supper, His throat, mouth, tongue and lips were terribly parched. As a sacrifice, and so as not to lessen the pain, He had barely tasted the spiced and bitter wine which was offered to Him as an act of charity. How differently was the vinegar offered to Him now! This was used to revive those who fainted during their crucifixion so that they would continue to feel the pain. In the case of Our Lord, who had not fainted, the vinegar was offered in mockery. This additional suffering, He did not refuse. By His example, He teaches us how we ought to accept the sufferings which Providence permits others to inflict upon us. He also shows us the importance of mortifying our sense of taste.

The particular sins which Jesus atoned for by this suffering are intemperance, gluttony and sins of the tongue. As we meditate upon the vinegar, we also recall the thirst of Jesus for love and for souls. Today let us do all we can to quench this thirst, and to atone for sins of the tongue. We could perhaps try to refrain from drinking between meal times as a way of showing our compassion for Jesus.

Prayers

Eternal Father, in reparation for sins of intemperance, gluttony, and all sins of the tongue, I offer Thee all the sufferings which Jesus endured in His sense of taste, particularly in taking the vinegar.

O Jesus, I wish to quench Thy thirst, not with vinegar, but with love and with souls.

Thursday First Week in Lent

Tongues of the Blasphemers–Sense of Hearing

Blaspheming tongues abounded then,
But now they're everywhere;
And many are the sins of men
Who in this evil share.

For those who mock the Faith today
And those who sin by hearing,
Let us atone; and watch and pray
For blasphemy repairing.

"How long, O God, shall the enemy reproach: is the adversary to provoke thy name forever? ... Remember this, the enemy hath reproached the Lord: and a foolish people hath provoked thy name."

—Psalm 73:10,18

"For thy iniquity hath taught thy mouth, and thou imitatest the tongue of blasphemers."

—Job 15:5

"Woe to the sinful nation, a people laden with iniquity, a wicked seed, ungracious children: they have forsaken the Lord, they have blasphemed the Holy One of Israel, they are gone away backwards."

—Isaias 1:4

"Whom hast thou reproached, and whom hast thou blasphemed, and against whom hast thou exalted thy voice, and lifted up thy eyes on high? Against the Holy One of Israel."

—Isaias 37:23

"My name is continually blasphemed all the day long."

—Isaias 52:5

"... let us strike him with the tongue, and let us give no heed to all his words."

—Jeremias 18:18

"And they that passed by, blasphemed him, wagging their heads."

—Matthew 27:39

"And one of those robbers who were hanged, blasphemed him, saying: If thou be Christ, save thyself and us."

—Luke 23:39

Meditation

All throughout His public life, Jesus had suffered when hearing Himself accused of blasphemy, and when encountering the mockery and unbelief of the scribes and Pharisees. His Passion evoked no sympathy, but rather abundant torrents of blasphemy both from them and from the soldiers. Consider the pain it must have caused Him to find many of His creatures so ungrateful for the great gift of Redemption which He was offering them at so great a cost to Himself; while knowing that thereby they were incurring the wrath and justice of His Father. Many, perhaps, at least among the soldiers, blasphemed the Lord in ignorance of Who He really was; but today, how many can be excused on the grounds of ignorance?

Jesus suffered in His sense of hearing, not only for all those who make a mockery of Religion, but also for sins of hearing such as are incurred by willingly listening to bad music, slander, detraction, false teachers and so on. Let us join Him today in making reparation for these sins, both by reverently invoking His Holy Name, and by mortifying our sense of hearing in some way.

Prayers

Eternal Father, I offer Thee all the sufferings of Jesus in His sense of hearing, especially during His Sacred Passion, in reparation for those who make a mockery of religion and for all sins of hearing.

May our prayers rise up before Thee to console Thee, O Lord, for all the blasphemies during Thy Sacred Passion and from the beginning till the end of time.

Blessed be the Name of the Lord!

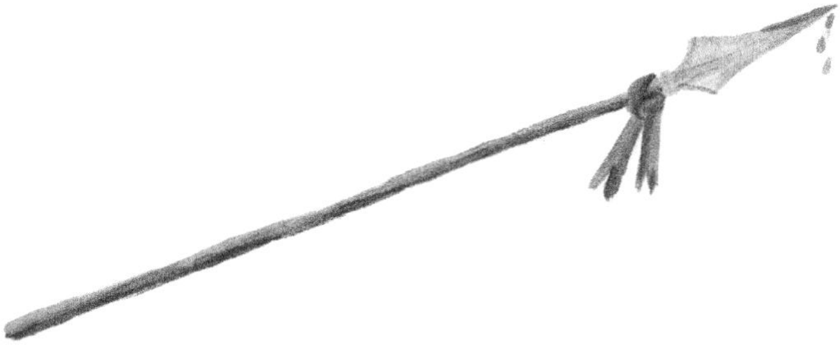

Friday First Week in Lent

Feast of the Holy Lance

A soldier opened, with a lance,
Christ's Sacred Heart and Side;
Our Lady watched, with anguished glance,
This instrument applied.

Her Heart, like His, is pierced anew
By sinners everywhere;
Console them then this whole day through
For all sins of despair.

"My sorrow is above sorrow, my heart mourneth within me."
—Jeremias 8:18

"And I will pour out upon the house of David, and upon the inhabitants of Jerusalem, the spirit of grace, and of prayers: and they shall look upon me, whom they have pierced: and they shall mourn for him as one mourneth for an only son, and they shall grieve over him, as the manner is to grieve for the death of the firstborn."
—Zacharias 12:10

"The sun and the moon stood still in their habitation, in the light of thy arrows, they shall go in the brightness of thy glittering spear."
—Habacuc 3:11

"And when they were going forth together with a willing mind, there appeared at Jerusalem a horseman going before them in white clothing, with golden armour, shaking a spear."
—2 Machabees 11:8

"But one of the soldiers with a spear opened his side, and immediately there came out blood and water."
—John 19:34

"And again another scripture saith: They shall look on him whom they pierced."
—John 19:37

Meditation

In contemplating the Passion of Jesus, we must not overlook the compassion of Mary. When the soldier opened the side of Jesus with a lance and pierced His Sacred Heart, Jesus Himself was already dead and could no longer feel the pain, but His Mother felt it keenly. This was the fulfilment of Simeon's prophecy, when the sword of sorrow pierced Our Lady's soul. St. Bernard of Clairvaux mentions in one of his sermons that the spear could not pierce the Body of Jesus without piercing Mary's heart. His soul had already departed, but her soul could not be torn away. This also fulfilled the prophecy of Zacharias: They shall look upon Me whom they have pierced.

If the Side of Jesus had not been opened thus, who would have known the extent of His love which sacrificed everything for us, even to the shedding of the last drop of Blood? Who would have dared to seek refuge in His Sacred Heart if the way had not been opened? And yet how poorly has this tremendous love been repaid!

Let us make reparation today for those who despise the love of Jesus and Mary, piercing their Hearts anew by sin. Let us especially make reparation for sins of despair which are so painful to these Hearts, and ever strive to acquire perfect love of God which is the greatest recompense we can give them.

Prayers

Eternal Father, I offer Thee the sorrow of Mary when the Side of Jesus was opened with a lance. By Thy great love thus revealed, I beg Thee to have mercy on those who continue to pierce the Hearts of Jesus and Mary anew, especially by sins of despair.

May the Holy Lance which pierced Thy Sacred Heart, O Jesus, pierce our hearts too with perfect contrition and love for Thee.

Saturday First Week in Lent

Spices—Sense of Smell

Some saints could smell the stench of sin;
The Saint of saints as well.
The spices which they wrapped Him in
Recall the sense of smell.

A pleasing scent of recompense
Your fervent prayers shall be,
For all His sufferings in this sense;
And sins of vanity.

"Spikenard and saffron, sweet cane and cinnamon, with all the trees of Libanus, myrrh and aloes with all the chief perfumes."
—Canticle of Canticles 4:14

"I have perfumed my bed with myrrh, aloes, and cinnamon."
—Proverbs 7:17

"Now there were some that had indignation within themselves, and said: Why was this waste of the ointment made?"
—Mark 14:4

"And returning, they prepared spices and ointments; and on the sabbath day they rested, according to the commandment."
—Luke 23:56

"Mary therefore took a pound of ointment of right spikenard, of great price, and anointed the feet of Jesus, and wiped his feet with her hair; and the house was filled with the odour of the ointment."
—John 12:3

"And Nicodemus also came, (he who at the first came to Jesus by night,) bringing a mixture of myrrh and aloes, about an hundred pound weight."
—John 19:39

Meditation

Some of the Saints could smell the bad odour of sin. Our Lord surely did so as well, especially in His Passion when He was surrounded by wicked men. He also experienced a horrible physical stench during the night of His arrest when He was lowered into a filthy dungeon. In memory of these outrages and to compassionate Our Lord for all the sufferings He endured in His sense of smell, we meditate on the spices as the instrument of His Sacred Passion.

While Joseph of Arimathea was beseeching Pilate for the body of Jesus, Nicodemus arrived on Calvary, bringing with him about a hundred Roman pounds (72 modern pounds or 33 kg) of a costly mixture of myrrh and aloes. Jesus' body was wrapped in linen cloths containing these spices, according to the Jewish burial custom. These spices were not a torment, but rather a consolation for Jesus, as was the precious ointment with which he was anointed by Mary Magdalene. They were part of the first reparation made to Him for the outrages of His Passion.

Today there is, if possible, an even greater need for reparation than ever before. The Church, Christ's Mystical Body, is likewise being tortured by Her enemies, and is passing through Her own Passion, while the world is full of the stench of sin. Let us make special efforts today to console our Blessed Lord by our prayers, acts of love, and the pleasing fragrance of virtue for all the sufferings He endured in the sense of smell and also in reparation for sins of vanity.

Prayers

Eternal Father, I offer Thee the fragrant spices with which Jesus was buried and all the prayers of Thy faithful, in reparation for sins of vanity and for all those who yield the bad odour of sin.

May our prayers rise up before Thee as a pleasing fragrance, O Jesus, and console Thee for all Thy sufferings in Thy sense of smell.

Second Sunday in Lent

Flaming Torches

The flaming torches call to mind
The fire of Faith and Love;
So needful to assist mankind
To reach our home above.

Yet darkness fills the earth today,
Since men reject the Light;
Let us for Mary's Triumph pray
To end this awful night.

"And Elias the prophet stood up, as a fire, and his word burnt like a torch."

—Ecclesiasticus 48:1

"And the light shineth in darkness, and the darkness did not comprehend it."

—John 1.5

"Again therefore, Jesus spoke to them, saying: I am the light of the world: he that followeth me, walketh not in darkness, but shall have the light of life."

—John 8:12

"Judas therefore having received a band of soldiers and servants from the chief priests and the Pharisees, cometh thither with lanterns and torches and weapons."

—John 18:3

Meditation

As we contemplate the flaming torches used to arrest Jesus in the Garden of Gethsemane, let us recall that fire is a symbol of faith and also of charity. When either of these virtues is lacking, the light of truth is obstructed and darkness ensues. A great darkness envelops the world today. Even former Catholic countries like Ireland and France, who brought the light of Faith to pagan nations down through the centuries, are now shrouded in the thick darkness of apostasy and indifferentism. The fiery torch is symbolic of the preacher who brings the light of faith to others, but how rare are preachers of truth at the present time! For want of a practical and living faith (as opposed to a merely verbal or intellectual belief) charity has grown cold, leaving many souls without a beacon to guide them to their eternal home.

When Our Lord was arrested, despite the flaming torches which they carried, those who accompanied Judas were in darkness, although the Light of the World stood in their midst. To this day numerous souls remain in spiritual darkness, despite their visible lights of fame, power and temporal goods, while in the physical darkness of the tabernacle, the Light of the World dwells continually; abandoned, forgotten and ignored by many.

Let us endeavour to make reparation today for those who have lost or who are lacking in faith and charity. As we pray that this fire will be rekindled both in our own country and throughout the world, let us also ask that it may be increased in our own heart. If possible, let us pay a visit to Jesus in the Blessed Sacrament, and if we cannot do so in person, let us at least do so in spirit. This will console Him for the coldness and indifference of those who have lost faith in the Real Presence and who refuse to profit from the Redemption He purchased for us at so great a price.

Prayers

Eternal Father, I offer Thee all the sufferings of Jesus in His Passion especially in being arrested as a criminal, in reparation for sins against faith and charity by which men reject the Light.

O Jesus, may the fire of faith and charity be rekindled in those hearts which have grown cold, and increased in those hearts which are warm.

Monday Second Week in Lent

Holy Sepulchre

The sepulchre where Christ reposed
We contemplate today;
Atoning for sins undisclosed,
And souls in sad decay.

By keeping in the state of grace
And praying much as well,
Our heart shall be a resting place
Where God will gladly dwell.

"And he laid his dead body in his own sepulchre: and they mourned over him, saying: Alas! alas! my brother. And when they had mourned over him, he said to his sons: When I am dead, bury me in the sepulchre wherein the man of God is buried: lay my bones beside his bones."

—3 Kings 13:30-31

"In that day the root of Jesse, who standeth for an ensign of the people, him the Gentiles shall beseech, and his sepulchre shall be glorious."

—Isaias 11:10

"Now there was in the place where he was crucified, a garden; and in the garden a new sepulchre, wherein no man yet had been laid. There, therefore, because of the parasceve of the Jews, they laid Jesus, because the sepulchre was nigh at hand."

—John 19:41,42

"And when they had fulfilled all things that were written of him, taking him down from the tree, they laid him in a sepulchre."

—Acts 13:29

"For we are buried together with him by baptism into death; that as Christ is risen from the dead by the glory of the Father, so we also may walk in newness of life."

—Romans 6:4

Meditation

Let us contemplate today the sorrow and solitude of Mary when Jesus was laid in the tomb; recalling also the virtues of faith and hope with which she awaited the Resurrection. Today her sorrow is renewed at the sight of all those souls from whom the life of grace has been forced to depart. The whited sepulchres of which Our Lord spoke (namely hypocrites who strive to appear better in the eyes of others than they really are) are no less a grief for her motherly heart. We think in particular of grave sins which are deliberately concealed, resulting in the sacrilegious reception of the Sacraments. In reparation for those sins which have caused her such grief, and especially for all unworthy Communions, let us make our own heart a pleasant resting place for Our Lord and beg Him to make the enclosed garden of our soul fragrant with the perfume of those virtues of which we are most in need. And let us not be surprised if after all our efforts, Jesus seems to be dead within us. He is meanwhile bringing light and grace to souls who, like the souls in Limbo, have long dwelt in darkness. By accepting aridity, desolation and spiritual trials with resignation to His holy will, we learn to love Him for His own sake rather than for the sake of His gifts. By so doing, we leave Him free to use us as His instruments to draw many other souls to Himself, and thus we participate in His work of Redemption. As it was by dying that He destroyed our death, so it is also that by dying to ourselves, we shall find new life in Him.

Prayers

Eternal Father, I offer Thee the Faith, Hope and sorrow of Mary when Jesus was in the tomb, in reparation for souls in whom Thy grace is dead, and for all hidden sins which corrupt those souls who communicate unworthily.

O Jesus, help us to practice the virtues which please Thee most, so that our hearts may be a pleasant resting place for Thee.

Tuesday Second Week in Lent

Spittle

They treated Christ with great contempt:
They spat, despising grace;
Yet meekly He did not attempt
To turn away His Face.

O strive to wipe the spit away
By loving reparation,
For blasphemies abound today
In every land and nation.

"They abhor me, and flee far from me, and are not afraid to spit in my face."

—Job 30:10

"I have given my body to the strikers, and my cheeks to them that plucked them: I have not turned away my face from them that rebuked me, and spit upon me."

—Isaias 50:6

"But the things which proceed out of the mouth, come forth from the heart, and those things defile a man. For from the heart come forth evil thoughts, murders, adulteries, fornications, thefts, false testimonies, blasphemies."

—Matthew 15:18,19

"Then did they spit in his face, and buffeted him: and others struck his face with the palms of their hands."

—Matthew 26:67

"And spitting upon him, they took the reed, and struck his head."

—Matthew 27:30

"And they shall mock him, and spit on him, and scourge him, and kill him: and the third day he shall rise again."

—Mark 10:34

"For he shall be delivered to the Gentiles, and shall be mocked, and scourged, and spit upon."

—Luke 18:32

Meditation

Today we contemplate how the Sacred Face of Jesus was disfigured with spittle. When Our Lord foretold His Passion to His disciples, one of the few torments which He mentioned was that of being spat upon. Among the Jews, this was the highest form of contempt, and Jesus Who was God as well as man, felt this insult to His Sacred Person much more keenly than we can possibly imagine. To spit in the face of one's brother or friend would be bad enough, but to spit in the face of a loving father, a merciful benefactor, or a just king would be almost unforgivable and worthy of severe punishment. How much greater an evil it is to spit in the Face of God... and yet people do so countless times a day by sins of blasphemy.

Jesus revealed to Sr. Mary of St. Peter that all those who make reparation perform for Him the same service that Veronica did in offering Him her veil with which to wipe away the spittle. Today we shall strive to console Him especially for all the sins and blasphemies which proceed from the mouth and from the malice of evil hearts. With this intention, let us offer up some extra prayers of reparation using frequent ejaculations throughout the day and lovingly invoking His Name in all our difficulties.

Prayers

Eternal Father, I offer Thee the Holy Face of Jesus covered with spittle and subjected to every form of outrage in His Passion in reparation for those sins which proceed from the mouth and from evil hearts.

O Jesus, we offer Thee all the reparation made by faithful souls to console Thee for Thy sufferings in being spat upon.

Wednesday Second Week in Lent

Cross

The cross which Baptism has placed
On every Catholic's brow,
Is seldom lovingly embraced
By anybody now.

While others scorn this saving sign,
Let us at least atone;
And, like our blessed Lord Divine,
With joy accept our own.

"And the Lord said to him: Go through the midst of the city, through the midst of Jerusalem: and mark Thau[9] upon the foreheads of the men that sigh, and mourn for all the abominations that are committed in the midst thereof"

— Ezechiel 9:4

"And he that taketh not up his cross, and followeth me, is not worthy of me."

—Matthew 10:38

"And he said to all: If any man will come after me, let him deny himself, and take up his cross daily, and follow me."

—Luke 9:23

"And bearing his own cross, he went forth to that place which is called Calvary, but in Hebrew Golgotha. …Now there stood by the cross of Jesus, his mother, and his mother's sister, Mary of Cleophas, and Mary Magdalen."

—John 19:17,25

"For many walk, of whom I have told you often (and now tell you weeping), that they are enemies of the cross of Christ; Whose end is destruction; whose God is their belly; and whose glory is in their shame; who mind earthly things."

—Philippians 3:18,19

"For the word of the cross, to them indeed that perish, is foolishness; but to them that are saved, that is, to us, it is the power of God."

—1 Corinthians 1:18

[9] Thau, or Tau, is the last letter in the Hebrew alphabet and in ancient Hebrew was written in the form of a cross. The symbolism and significance of this is striking.

Meditation

By virtue of His Passion, Our Lord has sanctified and transformed the cross, which was formerly a symbol of ignominy, into the precious sign of salvation. It is by the Sign of the Cross that we are baptised and become children of God. The cross of suffering is a token of God's love for us because of its power to make us more like Jesus Crucified. The children of the world instinctively flee from pain and suffering, but as children of God we learn to accept it and even treasure the cross as our means of salvation. The cross has always been the insignia of the Christian soldier, and it is by patiently carrying our daily cross that we manifest our loyalty to Jesus Christ. In the New Conciliar Church, the cross is frequently despised and has been treated with the greatest irreverence. It has even been recorded that in a Catholic cathedral in Austria, a crucifix was turned upside down and used as a clock. In reparation for such horrible outrages as these, let us always make the Sign of the Cross with reverence and care. We can also offer the reparation made by faithful souls down through the centuries and especially the merits of the Sacred Passion to appease God's justice, which is provoked so much today by those who revile the cross of Christ.

Prayers

Eternal Father, I offer Thee the Cross of Our Lord Jesus Christ and all the other instruments of His Holy Passion as weapons with which to drive from Thy Church the horrible sin of blasphemy.

We adore Thee O Christ and we bless Thee, because by Thy Holy Cross Thou hast redeemed the world.

Thursday Second Week in Lent

Ropes and Chains

They bound Our Lord with ropes and chains;
He let Himself be led;
But it is love which best explains
The meekness of our Head.

As far as circumstance allows,
Let us atone today,
For those untrue to marriage vows,
And all who disobey.

"They humbled his feet in fetters: the iron pierced his soul."

—Psalm 104:18

"The steps of man are guided by the Lord: but who is the man that can understand his own way? It is ruin to a man to devour holy ones, and after vows to retract."

—Proverbs 20:24-25

"And they brought him bound, and delivered him to Pontius Pilate the governor."

—Matthew 27:2

"Again therefore he asked them: Whom seek ye? And they said, Jesus of Nazareth. Jesus answered, I have told you that I am he. If therefore you seek me, let these go their way… Then the band and the tribune, and the servants of the Jews, took Jesus, and bound him: And they led him away…"

—John 18:7-8,12-13

"But to them that are married, not I but the Lord command-eth, that the wife depart not from her husband. And if she depart, that she remain unmarried, or be reconciled to her husband. And let not the husband put away his wife"

—1 Corinthians 7:10-11

Meditation

Today we contemplate Our Lord Jesus taken as a prisoner and bound with ropes and chains. From the moment when He was arrested as a criminal in the Garden of Gethsemane to the moment He was taken down from the cross, Jesus remained bound in some way or another. Led from one magistrate to another and roughly pulled in every direction, Our Lord offered no resistance. Behold how He atones for sins of disobedience, by becoming obedient even unto the death of the cross!

Bound with heavy chains in a filthy prison for several hours, tied to the pillar so tightly that his skin was broken, bound as the soldiers led Him to Calvary, and finally bound to the cross with nails, Jesus atoned by these sufferings for those who are unfaithful to their marriage vows. He shows us how seriously we are to take the words "until death do us part;" for He remained bound until death, although it was love more than anything else which caused Him to allow Himself to be bound by ropes and chains. And even in death, Jesus was bound with linen cloths. Behold our example!

Whatever be our state in life, let us implore Our Lord for the grace of binding ourselves to Him by greater fidelity to the duties of our state, and by a supernatural love which will enable us to accept with meekness and patience the difficulties we encounter. This will be easier to do if we consider ourselves as voluntarily bound along with Jesus, and follow wholeheartedly, as He did, the path traced out for us by Divine Providence. Today we shall perform our duties carefully and lovingly to make reparation for all those unfaithful to their marriage vows, and for all sins of disobedience.

Prayers

Eternal Father, I offer Thee all the ropes and chains with which Jesus was bound in His Sacred Passion and also the obedience of those who keep Thy commandments, in reparation for those unfaithful to their marriage vows and for sins of disobedience.

O Jesus, may Thy great love for mankind which kept Thee bound during Thy Passion bind the power of Satan and draw many souls to Thyself.

Friday Second Week in Lent

Feast of the Holy Shroud

Christ's Body, shrouded like the dead,
Lay hid from every eye.
Today beneath the form of bread,
Divinity doth lie.

For love of men He has endured
Extremes of profanation.
Your love and reverence shall afford
His Heart much consolation.

"Our soul is dry, our eyes behold nothing else but manna."
—Numbers 11:6

"Despised, and the most abject of men, a man of sorrows, and acquainted with infirmity: and his look was as it were hidden and despised, whereupon we esteemed him not."
—Isaias 53:3

"And Joseph taking the body, wrapped it up in a clean linen cloth."
—Matthew 27:59

"And Joseph buying fine linen, and taking him down, wrapped him up in the fine linen, and laid him in a sepulchre which was hewed out of a rock."
—Mark 15:26

"They took therefore the body of Jesus, and bound it in linen cloths, with the spices, as the manner of the Jews is to bury."
—John 19:40

"And when he stooped down, he saw the linen cloths lying; but yet he went not in. Then cometh Simon Peter, following him, and went into the sepulchre, and saw the linen cloths lying, And the napkin that had been about his head, not lying with the linen cloths, but apart, wrapped up into one place."
—John 20:5-7

Meditation

The Shroud which concealed the Body of Jesus from the gaze of all, even from those who loved Him most, is like the little white Host in which Jesus is truly present, though His human form is concealed. Because He is not seen under the same appearances which were seen by His friends on Good Friday, how many people have doubted His Real Presence, or shown by their conduct and their irreverence that they do not believe the consecrated Host to be anything more than blessed bread? As a result of this lack of faith, how many profanations have taken place in those churches where Our Lord reposes? When the Hosts have been validly consecrated, He is hidden in the tabernacle as He was hidden in the sepulchre, unseen by men, yet truly present: Body, Blood, Soul and Divinity! In reparation for the lack of reverence which is shown to our Eucharistic Lord, let us offer Him our love and the love of all faithful souls to surround Him and console Him as the Shroud did on that first Good Friday. We can also console Him by visiting Him often, at least in spirit, in the Sacrament of His Love; and by making our heart a living tabernacle where He will always find a warm and loving welcome. We should cherish a lively devotion to Jesus in the Blessed Sacrament and act in all things, not according to what we see, but according to what we profess to believe regarding His Real Presence in the Holy Eucharist.

Prayers

Eternal Father, I offer Thee the Holy Face of Jesus, hidden in the Eucharist, in reparation for all those who treat the Most Blessed Sacrament with irreverence, and for all profanations of Thy holy Churches.

O Jesus, hidden in the Blessed Sacrament, I adore Thee, and I offer Thee my love and the love of all faithful souls to console Thee for all the outrages Thou receivest in this Mystery.

Saturday Second Week in Lent

Scarlet Cloak

The soldiers used it for a joke
To dress Him as a king.
Christ's Precious Blood, His scarlet cloak,
Became a sacred thing.

For sins so rampant in these times:
Confessions badly made,
Abortion, murder, and such crimes—
For these was Christ arrayed.

"And then come, and accuse me, saith the Lord: if your sins be as scarlet, they shall be made as white as snow: and if they be red as crimson, they shall be white as wool."

—Isaias 1:18

"And stripping him, they put a scarlet cloak about him... And after they had mocked him, they took off the cloak from him, and put on him his own garments, and led him away to crucify him."

—Matthew 27:28,31

"And they clothe him with purple, and platting a crown of thorns, they put it upon him... And after they had mocked him, they took off the purple from him, and put his own garments on him, and they led him out to crucify him."

—Mark 15:17,20

"Blessed are they that wash their robes in the blood of the Lamb: that they may have a right to the tree of life, and may enter in by the gates into the city."

—Apocalypse 22:14

Meditation

The scarlet cloak which we read about in the Gospel according to St. Matthew, is referred to as purple by St. Mark. Scarlet and purple are often used together in Holy Scripture and some commentators hold that the Hebrew word refers to the same colour. In any case, the soldiers used this cloak to make a mockery of the Kingship of Christ. The scarlet cloak was symbolic of the royal robe of the Precious Blood, which is the richest robe that any king ever wore. It is at the same time also symbolic of the burden of our sins which Christ took upon Himself, as we may gather from the words of Isaias: if your sins be as scarlet, they shall be made as white as snow. By the scarlet cloak of His Most Precious Blood, the scarlet of our sins was blotted out. O Infinite Goodness and Infinite Justice of God, which found in this Royal Robe an admirable means of reconciliation!

By offering this priceless robe to the Eternal Father, let us atone for those who still mock our Lord Jesus Christ by refusing to have their sins blotted out through the Sacrament of Penance, in which the merits of the Precious Blood are applied to the soul. This mockery takes place, not only by refusing to approach the confessional, but also by wilfully concealing grave sins from the confessor or confessing them without contrition. Let us also make reparation for sins of wilful murder, especially abortions, which render so many mothers and doctors guilty of shedding innocent blood.

Prayers

Eternal Father, I offer Thee the Precious Blood of Jesus and the scarlet cloak with which He was clothed and mocked, in reparation for bad confessions and sins of murder.

O Jesus, may the scarlet cloak of Thy Precious Blood blot out our sins and make our souls whiter than snow.

Third Sunday in Lent

Fool's White Garment

Arrayed in white by Herod's men,
Much mocking Christ endured,
As faithful souls are mocked again
For following Our Lord.

For those from stain of sin set free
Beg grace to so remain;
Atoning for impurity,
And every mortal stain.

"At all times let thy garments be white, and let not oil depart from thy head."

—Ecclesiasticus 9:8

"And Herod with his army set him at nought, and mocked him, putting on him a white garment, and sent him back to Pilate."

—Luke 23:11

"But thou hast a few names in Sardis, which have not defiled their garments: and they shall walk with me in white, because they are worthy. He that shall overcome, shall thus be clothed in white garments, and I will not blot out his name out of the book of life, and I will confess his name before my Father, and before his angels."

—Apocalypse 3:4-5

"And one of the ancients answered, and said to me: These that are clothed in white robes, who are they? and whence came they? And I said to him: My Lord, thou knowest. And he said to me: These are they who are come out of great tribulation, and have washed their robes, and have made them white in the blood of the Lamb."

—Apocalypse 7:13-14

Meditation

At the time of the Passion, white garments were reserved for kings, rulers and priests. Jesus was clothed in white as a mock king by Herod, who had refused to amend his corrupt life. Jesus had no need to speak to Herod. His very presence was a silent reproach to the ruler, who must have known, like Pilate, that Jesus was innocent of the crimes laid to His charge. Herod had refused to obey the call to repentance when John the Baptist had rebuked him three years before; and since that time he had only become more accustomed to and hardened in his impure way of life. Yet even he proclaimed the innocence, kingship and priesthood of Jesus by causing him to be clothed in this symbolic white garment and by refusing to condemn Him.

How numerous are those who have sullied the white robe of sanctifying grace received at Baptism! Innocence and purity are virtues rarely found in modern-day society. Like our Blessed Lord, those who wear the white garment of grace are often mocked. Let us make reparation for those whose souls are stained by sins of impurity, so that they might regain the white robe of sanctifying grace; and beg that those who are free from such sins may always remain so.

Prayers

Eternal Father, I offer Thee the white robe of a fool with which Jesus was clothed by Herod, the merits He gained by it and the merits of all those who make themselves foolish in the eyes of the world for Thy sake, in reparation for those who have lost their white robe of purity and for all sins against this virtue.

O Jesus, I beg Thee to cleanse our souls in Thy Most Precious Blood so that they may shine with the whiteness of purity.

Monday Third Week in Lent

Chalice of Suffering

No suffering was more intense
Than that which Christ took up;
Foreseeing man's poor recompense,
He drained the bitter cup.

In tempted sufferers everywhere
By Faith let us behold Him;
Relieving them, we'll also share
The chalice which consoled Him.

"I will take the chalice of salvation; and I will call upon the name of the Lord."

—Psalm 115:137

"And Jesus answering, said: You know not what you ask. Can you drink the chalice that I shall drink? They say to him: We can."

—Matthew 20:22

"And he was withdrawn away from them a stone's cast; and kneeling down, he prayed, Saying: Father, if thou wilt, remove this chalice from me: but yet not my will, but thine be done. And there appeared to him an angel from heaven, strengthening him. And being in an agony, he prayed the longer."

—Luke 22:41-43

"Jesus therefore said to Peter: Put up thy sword into the scabbard. The chalice which my Father hath given me, shall I not drink it?"

—John 18:11

Meditation

Archbishop Fulton Sheen points out in one of his conferences that Our Lady was asked at the Annunciation whether she would make it possible for God to suffer by giving Him a human nature. She knew that as His Mother she would suffer immensely too, yet her 'Fiat' foreshadowed that of her Son: 'Thy will be done.' In His agony, Jesus abandoned Himself to the will of the Father, although He was overwhelmed by the bitterness of the Passion which He was asked to endure for the Redemption of humanity.

One of the greatest sufferings which were contained in the bitter chalice He was asked to drink was the knowledge that for so many souls, His Passion would profit nothing. Nay, it would rather increase their guilt because of the magnitude of malice involved in refusing the grace of salvation, which would be purchased and offered to them at such a cost. Added to this distressing thought was the knowledge of how, even among His own, His love would be repaid so poorly. So much coldness, indifference, lukewarmness, and lack of generosity! So many souls who would offer Him only a divided heart... But the Angel brought Him a chalice of strength, reminding Him of the multitudes who would profit from being raised from the death of sin to a life of grace; as well as the fervent souls who would strive their utmost to repay His love. O let us pray that we may be among this latter number of souls, who formed the chalice of strength! And let us pray also for those who are enduring great trials and temptations, lest they be unfaithful to grace and add to the bitterness of the chalice of suffering.

Prayers

Eternal Father, may the chalice of suffering which Thy Divine Son received and which is shared by faithful souls, be turned into a chalice of strength for those in temptation.

O Jesus, may the souls whom Thou hast saved by Thy Precious Blood, console Thee for all those who refuse to be saved and upon whom Thy grace is poured in vain.

Tuesday Third Week in Lent

Veil of Veronica

Veronica courageously
Went forth to meet the Lord.
Upon her veil shall ever be
Christ's Image – her reward.

The Face of Christ shall be impressed
Likewise on every heart
By whom He's fearlessly confessed;
Who dare to stand apart.

"They have heard that I sigh, and there is none to comfort me: all my enemies have heard of my evil, they have rejoiced that thou hast done it: thou hast brought a day of consolation, and they shall be like unto me."

—Lamentations 1:21

"And it shall come to pass that every one that shall see thee, shall flee from thee, and shall say: Ninive is laid waste: who shall bemoan thee? whence shall I seek a comforter for thee?"

—Nahum 3:7

"As one whom the mother caresseth, so will I comfort you, and you shall be comforted in Jerusalem."

—Isaias 66:13

"Behold, O God our protector: and look on the face of thy Christ."

—Psalm 83:10

"Now whosoever saw the countenance of the high priest, was wounded in heart: for his face, and the changing of his colour declared the inward sorrow of his mind."

—2 Machabees 3:16

Meditation

Today, perhaps more than at any other point in history, we witness a great need for reparation and for courageous Veronicas to step out from the crowd to console Our Lord. To be a Veronica means that we strive to become a true image of our Suffering Lord by reproducing His likeness in our souls. It requires us also to act out of love for the Suffering Christ and His Mystical Body, the Catholic Church; doing everything we can to console Him and to atone for the outrages and blasphemies to which He is everywhere subjected. To be a Veronica, we must disregard human respect in order to give Our Lord the respect which He deserves; and we may be sure that our reward will be great indeed. One would say at first glance that never was there a greater reward in all of history than that which Veronica received. Who could ever be given a cloth more precious than that veil in recompense for an act of courage and love? But there is a grace which is more valuable than having the Holy Face of our Saviour stamped on a veil. To have the likeness of Christ impressed upon our hearts is a privilege which far surpasses Veronica's reward; for if we keep this Image free from stain of mortal sin, it is a token of everlasting life and a happy assurance that we shall behold the Glorious Face of our God forever in the Beatific Vision.

Let us offer this veil (and more importantly, the image upon it—the Holy Face of Jesus) to the Eternal Father. This holy Icon will not only console Him, but will draw down special graces upon the souls who offend Him by blasphemy. The veil of Veronica and the Holy Face will thus act as a shield to draw down mercy rather than justice upon these souls.

Prayers

Eternal Father, I offer Thee the veil of Veronica and the Holy Face of Jesus impressed upon it in reparation for blasphemy.

Look not upon Thy guilty people, O God, but upon the Face of Thy Beloved Son, and have mercy on us for His sake.

Behold, O God, our Protector, and look on the Face of Thy Christ!

Wednesday Third Week in Lent

Reed

They took a reed and struck His Head;
As a sceptre used this rod.
They owed Him honour, but instead
They mocked the Lamb of God.

Atone for man's abuse of power,
In Church as well as state;
And for the weak who in this hour
With such cooperate.

“Thy throne, O God, is forever and ever: the sceptre of thy kingdom is a sceptre of uprightness.”

—Psalm 44:7

“. . . with a rod shall they strike the cheek of the judge of Israel.”

—Micheas 5:1

“The Lord hath broken the staff of the wicked, the rod of the rulers, That struck the people in wrath with an incurable wound, that brought nations under in fury, that persecuted in a cruel manner.”

—Isaias 14:5-6

“. . . for the wickedness of my people have I struck him.”

—Isaias 53:8

“And when they went their way, Jesus began to say to the multitudes concerning John: What went you out into the desert to see? a reed shaken with the wind?”

—Matthew 11:7

“And platting a crown of thorns, they put it upon his head, and a reed in his right hand. And bowing the knee before him, they mocked him, saying: Hail, king of the Jews. And spitting upon him, they took the reed, and struck his head.”

—Matthew 27:29-30

“And they struck his head with a reed: and they did spit on him. And bowing their knees, they adored him.”

—Mark 15:19

Meditation

Today, let us contemplate the reed which Our Lord was given as a mock sceptre and which was used by the soldiers to strike His Sacred Head. The reed can be compared to the rod of Aaron, which is symbolic of the priestly office. It is also a symbol of power and authority. The reed was the instrument used to drive the thorns deeper into the Head of Jesus, who took our iniquities upon Himself and suffered for the sins of us all. At the present time within Church and State, we are witnessing a repetition of those in positions of authority misusing their power to increase the sufferings of Christ in His Mystical Body. We also behold many who are morally weak, like reeds shaken by the wind, participating in the sins of bad leaders and co-operating with unjust and immoral laws for fear of being criticised. There were probably many among the soldiers who, if left to themselves, would not have taken pleasure in such cruelty; yet human respect overcame the voice of conscience, and they also took part in mocking Our Lord. As we meditate on His sufferings in being struck with the reed, let us pray for the moral courage to follow our conscience, in spite of the opposition which we may meet with from a disapproving crowd. Let us also atone in whatever way we can for the moral weakness which is so prevalent today; perhaps by denying ourselves some legitimate pleasure.

Prayers

Eternal Father, I offer Thee all the sufferings of Jesus in His Passion, especially those He received by the reed, in reparation for those who misuse their authority and for all those who are morally weak.

O Jesus, we beg Thee to strengthen our human frailty by Thy grace so that we may overcome all human respect and courageously do whatever Thou wouldst have us to do.

Thursday Third Week in Lent

Pillar

Bound to the pillar, and savagely lashed,
Brought time after time to the ground,
Christ struggled to rise, though deeply gashed,
And strength in the pillar found.

Trusting in the pillar of the strength of Christ,
Let us bravely struggle on,
To prevent the Faith being sacrificed
Where the clerical pillars are gone.

"And the Lord went before them to shew the way by day in a pillar of a cloud, and by night in a pillar of fire: that he might be the guide of their journey at both times."

—Exodus 13:21

"He said: Let me die with the Philistines. And when he had strongly shook the pillars, the house fell upon all the princes, and the rest of the multitude that was there: and he killed many more at his death, than he had killed before in his life."

—Judges 16:30

"The Lord is the strength of his people, and the protector of the salvation of his anointed."

—Psalm 27:8

"And when James, Cephas, and John, who seemed to be pillars, perceived the grace that was given unto me, they gave to me and Barnabas the right hands of fellowship; that we should go unto the heathen, and they unto the circumcision."

—Galatians 2:9

"He that shall overcome, I will make him a pillar in the temple of my God."

—Apocalypse 3:12

Meditation

The pillar appears frequently in the pages of Holy Scripture. We read of the pillar of cloud and of fire; a symbol of God's presence among His chosen people and of His fatherly care for them. Samson was fastened between two pillars, and died by destroying them so that the roof fell upon the Philistines. In this he was a figure of Christ, who died with outstretched arms, and by His death brought deliverance to God's people. In His Passion Our Lord was bound to a pillar during the cruel scourging to which He was subjected. He used this pillar as a means of pulling Himself up again when He had been beaten down to the ground by the cruel blows He received. This scene is shown very clearly in the movie 'The Passion of the Christ' by Mel Gibson.

In our weakness, we have great need to remember that Our Lord is a pillar of strength to those who trust in Him. Even if we are scourged by trials and troubles, let us cling to Him as a sure support, knowing that He will never fail us. So long as we are doing His will, we know that we can count on His strength to sustain us and help us to reach our eternal home, even when those on whom we should have been able to depend let us down. As we meditate on the pillar, let us not forget to pray for those members of the clergy who should be pillars of strength, upholding the Church as the apostles did, but who have failed in their duty. We can help to make up for their failure by greater fidelity to our own duties. This is the universal path to sanctity. Since the entire Church benefits from the holiness of each of Her members, it is also an excellent way of making reparation.

Prayers

Eternal Father, may the merits and the memory of the Passion of Thy Son support Thy Church in these evil times and atone for those members of the clergy who have failed in their duty of upholding the Faith.

We beg Thee, O Jesus, to be a pillar of strength to us and uphold us in this hour of the Passion of Thy Church.

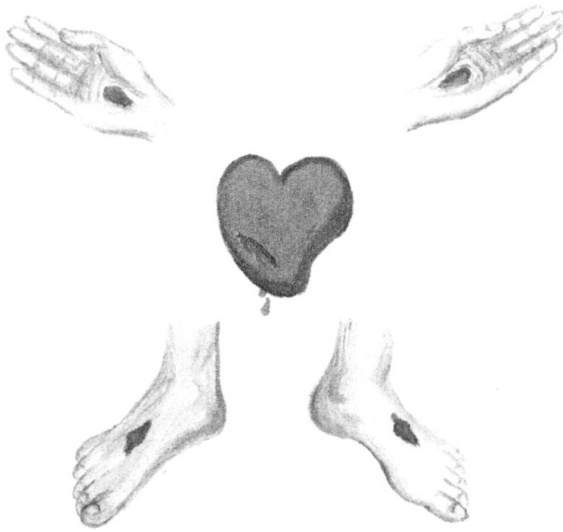

Friday Third Week in Lent

Feast of the Holy Wounds

As saving fountains opened wide
Whence Precious Blood doth flow,
Behold His Hands, His Feet, His Side;
His other Wounds also.

Through these most Holy Wounds, appeal
As often as you can
That God Himself would deign to heal
The wounds on souls of man.

"He hath torn me with wound upon wound, he hath rushed in upon me like a giant"

—Job 16:15

"For many dogs have encompassed me: the council of the malignant hath besieged me. They have dug my hands and feet."

—Psalm 21:17

"Because they have persecuted him whom thou hast smitten; and they have added to the grief of my wounds."

—Psalm 68:27

"From the sole of the foot unto the top of the head, there is no soundness therein: wounds and bruises and swelling sores: they are not bound up, nor dressed, nor fomented with oil."

—Isaias 1:6

"But he was wounded for our iniquities, he was bruised for our sins: the chastisement of our peace was upon him, and by his bruises we are healed."

—Isaias 53:5

"And they shall say to him: What are these wounds in the midst of thy hands? And he shall say: With these I was wounded in the house of them that loved me."

—Zacharias 13:6

Meditation

In the words of the Prophet Zacharias, we learn the cause of Our Lord's greatest sufferings: namely, the sins of those who profess they love Him, and yet who deny Him in practice. At the time of the Crucifixion, it was the Jews who had rejected Him and to whom this reproach was addressed, but now it is to Catholics all over the world that our Saviour addresses His loving complaint. Pope St. Pius X referred to this in his discourse on the beatification of St. Joan of Arc (13 December 1908): *"In our days more than ever the main strength of evil men lies in the cowardice and weakness of those who are good, and all the vigour of Satan's reign lies in the weakness of Christians. Oh! if I were allowed, as the prophet Zacharias did in spirit, to ask the Divine Redeemer: What are these wounds are in the midst of Thy hands? the answer would not be doubtful: these have been given to me in the house of those who loved me; given by my friends, who have done nothing to defend me and who on every occasion have become accomplices of my opponents."*

Since our Saviour received these wounds in order to pay the price of our Redemption, let us not fail to make good use of this treasure which has been placed at our disposal. By offering these Holy Wounds of Jesus to the Eternal Father, we may participate in saving many souls who would otherwise be lost for want of another chance.

Let us make reparation today for all sins in general, (including the sins being atoned for in Purgatory) by using the approved and indulgenced invocations revealed by Our Lord to Sr. Mary Martha Chambon, a holy Visitation nun.

Prayers

Eternal Father, I offer Thee the Wounds of Our Lord Jesus Christ to heal the wounds of our souls. *(300 days each time)*

My Jesus pardon and mercy through the merits of Thy Holy Wounds. *(300 days each time)*

Saturday Third Week in Lent

Hammer

The hammer's sound was often heard
For three-and-thirty years,
Until the final blows occurred,
In which the sinner shares.

Atone for broken vows today;
Be faithful to your own;
Amend your life without delay
If careless you have grown.

"If thou hast vowed any thing to God, defer not to pay it: for an unfaithful and foolish promise displeaseth him: but whatsoever thou hast vowed, pay it. And it is much better not to vow, than after a vow not to perform the things promised."

—Ecclesiastes 5:3-4

"The noise of the hammer is always in his ears, and his eye is upon the pattern of the vessel he maketh... But they shall strengthen the state of the world, and their prayer shall be in the work of their craft, applying their soul, and searching in the law of the most High."

—Ecclesiasticus 38:30,39

"It is no good thing to do hurt to the just: nor to strike the prince, who judgeth right."

—Proverbs 17:26

"He was taken away from distress, and from judgment: who shall declare his generation? because he is cut off out of the land of the living: for the wickedness of my people have I struck him."

—Isaias 53:8

"And when they were come to the place which is called Calvary, they crucified him there; and the robbers, one on the right hand, and the other on the left."

—Luke 23:33

Meditation

Jesus and St. Joseph worked together in Nazareth and it is easy to picture Jesus using the hammer while practicing the carpenter's trade. The sound of the hammer falling must been a constant reminder to Our Lord and Our Lady of the approaching Passion when again the hammer would fall, driving the nails into the Sacred Hands and Feet of our Saviour. The hammer is one of the instruments to which Our Lady of La Salette drew attention. As the hammer was used to drive the three nails into Our Lord's sacred hands and feet, it is symbolic of the pain inflicted on Our Lord by infidelity to the three vows of religion.

Those consecrated to God who are unfaithful to their sacred calling are the chief executioners who drive the nails into Christ's mystical Body. This has been especially true during the past six decades, when in the wake of Vatican II, the large majority of priests and religious embraced the worldly spirit. But they are not the only ones. Marriage vows and our baptismal vows are equally binding, and infidelity to these vows is also a source of suffering for Our Lord. Let us make special reparation today, in whatever way we are inspired to do so, for the sorrow caused to Jesus and Mary by broken vows and especially for the infidelity of priests and religious.

Prayers

Eternal Father, I offer Thee all the blows of the hammer which Jesus and Saint Joseph made in the workshop of Nazareth and those received by Jesus in His Sacred Passion, in reparation for all those who are unfaithful to their priestly vocation or religious vows.

May the fidelity of Thy faithful priests and religious console Thee, O Jesus, for all the hammer blows which Thou received when Thou wert nailed to the Cross.

Sunday Fourth Week in Lent

Lanterns

With lanterns came the guilty band,
Whose souls were dark as night;
In mortal sin, for, understand,
They had refused the Light.

For souls deep in the night of sin
We make amends today;
And we, by bearing Christ within,
Must strive to light their way.

"The lamp despised in the thoughts of the rich, is ready for the time appointed"

—Job 12:5

"Shall not the light of the wicked be extinguished, and the flame of his fire not shine? The light shall be dark in his tabernacle, and the lamp that is over him, shall be put out."

—Job 18:6

"For thou lightest my lamp, O Lord: O my God enlighten my darkness."

—Psalms 17:29

"Thy word is a lamp to my feet, and a light to my paths."

—Psalm 118:105

"Let your loins be girt, and lamps burning in your hands."

—Luke 12:35

"And the light shineth in darkness, and the darkness did not comprehend it."

—John 1:5

"Judas therefore having received a band of soldiers and servants from the chief priests and the Pharisees, cometh thither with lanterns and torches and weapons."

—John 18:3

Meditation

At the beginning of his Gospel, St. John gives a sublime description of Christ, the Light of the World and relates how "He came unto His own and His own received Him not." These words could well be written of people today. How many who ought to know Him, even among His own, neglect to receive Him when He descends upon the altar during Mass! How many are deaf to His holy inspirations by which He would willingly unite us to Himself so often during the day! Then there are souls like the scribes and Pharisees who know the truth but are afraid to inconvenience themselves by following it and so they continually expose themselves to the danger of losing the faith altogether. There are those who know and even admit that there is a God but deny Him in practice by neglecting to serve Him… Of all of these, and of us too, to some extent, it may be said that, "He came unto His own and His own received Him not."

We ourselves must be like lanterns, filled with the light of faith, hope and charity; and even more, with Christ Himself. He is the Light of the World, whom it is our duty to carry to others. Good example is especially powerful in leading others to Christ. If we have been enlightened by the true Light, it will shine through us and reveal to others the beauty of the Christian life. Let us take care not to hinder and obscure that light by voluntary infidelity to grace.

Prayers

Eternal Father, I offer Thee all the sufferings of Jesus in being rejected as the Light of the world in reparation for souls who have lost the faith and those in the darkness of mortal sin.

O Jesus, I beg Thee to fill my heart with the fire of Thy love so that I may be Thy lantern and bring Thee to all whom I meet.

May the light of Thy Face shine upon us O Lord!

Monday Fourth Week in Lent

Swords and Clubs

Though daily Jesus preached unharmed,
That night was Satan's hour.
With swords and clubs, the band was armed
Because they feared His power.

The Word of God and fervent prayer
Are arms which cannot fail
To guard the tempted souls who fear
To share in this betrayal.

"All holding swords, and most expert in war: every man's sword upon his thigh, because of fears in the night."
—Canticle of Canticles 3:8

"As he yet spoke, behold Judas, one of the twelve, came, and with him a great multitude with swords and clubs, sent from the chief priests and the ancients of the people."
—Matthew 26:47

"In that same hour Jesus said to the multitudes: You are come out as it were to a robber with swords and clubs to apprehend me. I sat daily with you, teaching in the temple, and you laid not hands on me."
—Matthew 26:55

"Begone Satan for it is written 'The Lord thy God shalt thou adore and Him only shalt thou serve.' And the devil left Him."
—Matthew 4:10,11

"And Jesus said to the chief priests, and magistrates of the temple, and the ancients, that were come unto him: Are ye come out, as it were against a thief, with swords and clubs?"
—Luke 22:52

"And take unto you the helmet of salvation, and the sword of the Spirit (which is the word of God)."
—Ephesians 6:17

Meditation

The multitude led by Judas who came to arrest Jesus was armed with swords and clubs because they feared the power of Jesus. This same power which caused such fear among the wicked is a source of joy to the just. We are weak, it is true, and our enemies are very many and very powerful; but the power of Jesus is greater. If we place our trust in Him then He will protect us from those who hate us and who seek to rob us of our most precious possessions – namely, our immortal soul and the garment of grace. The weapons of the Christian differ from the weapons used by those who arrested Jesus that night, for they are spiritual weapons. In former times, one of the most important weapons for every soldier was a sword. In modern-day warfare there many other more effective weapons, but in the spiritual battle, there are few things more necessary than the sword.

The Word of God is a sword – the sword of the spirit – with which we must always be armed; but especially in times of temptation. This is the weapon which Our Lord used to conquer Satan when He was tempted in the desert, and it is likewise the weapon we have been given to keep the devil at bay. We should often read and ponder on the words of Holy Scripture so that they will come easily to our minds when we have need of them.

Let us pray especially today for those in temptation so that they might have the grace to make use of the sword of the spirit – the Word of God – to overcome Satan and his cunning temptations.

Prayers

Eternal Father, I offer Thee the swords and clubs which were used to arrest Jesus, begging Thee to use them to put the devil to flight from those who are tempted.

Arise, O Lord, and may the sword of Thy Spirit, Thy holy Word, put to flight the devil and his temptations.

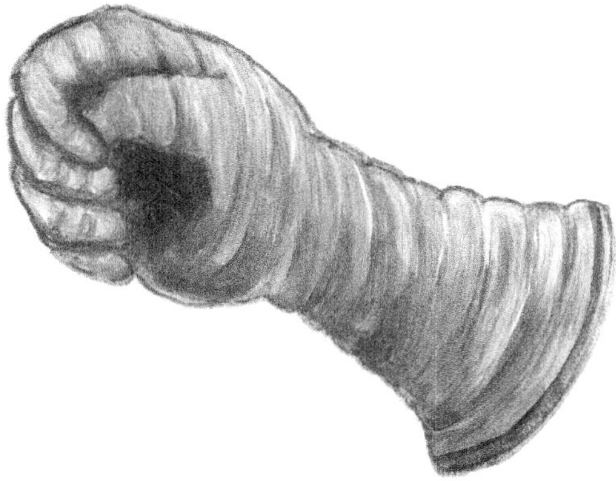

Tuesday Fourth Week in Lent

Gauntlet

Behold the gauntlet-covered hand
Which struck Christ's Holy Face:
A symbol of each sinner, and
Rejected truth and grace.

For infidels - the Church's foes,
And all apostatised,
Atone today; likewise for those
Whose Faith is compromised.

"It is no good thing to do hurt to the just: nor to strike the prince, who judgeth right."

—Proverbs 17:26

"Then did they spit in his face, and buffeted him: and others struck his face with the palms of their hands."

—Matthew 26:67

"And some began to spit on him, and to cover his face, and to buffet him, and to say unto him: Prophesy: and the servants struck him with the palms of their hands."

—Mark 14:65

"And the men that held him, mocked him, and struck him. And they blindfolded him, and smote his face. And they asked him, saying: Prophesy, who is it that struck thee?"

—Luke 22:63-64

"And when he had said these things, one of the servants standing by, gave Jesus a blow, saying: Answerest thou the high priest so?"

—John 18:22

Meditation

The other Evangelists record that Jesus was struck and mocked by the men who held Him, but St. John, who was the only Evangelist present at the time, only records the blow which Our Lord received from the servant of the high priest. This blow must therefore have impressed him greatly, not only because of the injustice of this action in response to the meek words of Jesus, but also because of the effect which it had upon the features of our Saviour. No doubt St. John also understood something of the pain which this blow inflicted upon the Heart of his Master. Consider how great was the insult of this action: The King of kings was struck by a mere servant; the blow was given in response to the words of truth which had just been uttered by Jesus, and in the presence of a large assembly of the religious leaders of the people. According to tradition, the servant's hand was covered with an iron gauntlet, making this blow much greater than it would have otherwise been.

As we meditate upon the meekness of Jesus and the way Truth Himself was treated by those hypocrites who pretended to be zealous for the law, let us beg for the grace to be equally meek and silently courageous when we are likewise disgraced before men and accused of being transgressors of the law. We must never forget that the law of God is supreme and that no earthly rulers have the power to enslave us by laws which contradict the laws of God.

Today let us make reparation for those who reject the Truth when it is manifested to them, and for those who sin by dishonesty, imploring our Lord to graciously extend His Hand to them and grant them the grace of sincere repentance.

Prayers

Eternal Father, I offer Thee all the blows which Jesus received from the hands of men during His Sacred Passion in reparation for those who reject the Truth and who thus continue to strike Him today.

O Jesus, may Thy Hand be mercifully extended to sinners to grant them the grace of repentance.

Wednesday Fourth Week in Lent

Cock/Rooster

The rooster crowed as Peter met
His Master's mournful gaze;
It calls those who deny Him yet
To mend their fallen ways.

We beg that those who hear the cock
May likewise use this chance
To come back to the Master's flock,
Converted by His glance.

"Jesus said to him: Amen I say to thee, that in this night before the cock crow, thou wilt deny me thrice."

—Matthew 26:34

"And he said: I say to thee, Peter, the cock shall not crow this day, till thou thrice deniest that thou knowest me… And Peter said: Man, I know not what thou sayest. And immediately, as he was yet speaking, the cock crew. And the Lord turning looked on Peter. And Peter remembered the word of the Lord, as he had said: Before the cock crow, thou shalt deny me thrice."

—Luke 22:34,60-61

"But if any man have not care of his own, and especially of those of his house, he hath denied the faith, and is worse than an infidel."

—1 Timothy 5:8

"For certain men are secretly entered in, (who were written of long ago unto this judgment,) ungodly men, turning the grace of our Lord God into riotousness, and denying the only sovereign Ruler, and our Lord Jesus Christ."

—Jude 1:4

Meditation

As faithful Catholics in the world of today, we are by our very presence and by our moral principles a cock crow for many people, reminding them of the Faith they have denied or the voice of conscience which they have ignored. Like Peter, some of these may deny Our Lord through weakness and fear, even though they do love Him. Many also, because the fire of charity has nearly become extinguished in their hearts, endeavour to warm themselves with the fire of their passions. All is not yet lost if we have been among that number! But let us be attentive to the glance of our Saviour and the crowing of the cock which call us to repentance. Let us not waste the grace which is given us, nor fall like Judas into despair, but hasten to Mary, the Refuge of Sinners, casting ourselves at her feet in tears of repentance. She will plead for us and obtain for us the mercy of her Divine Son.

While reflecting on these things, with true contrition for our own sins, let us make reparation for all those who deny Christ in thought, word and deed; especially for those who are baptised and fail to live up to their religious obligations. Let us readily forgive all those who have denied us or let us down in any way, so that we too may obtain forgiveness for the times when we have denied Christ by sin.

Prayers

Eternal Father, I offer Thee all the sufferings of Jesus when He was denied by Peter in reparation for those who deny Thee today, especially by infidelity to the Catholic faith.

O Jesus, as Thou didst turn and look upon Peter when the cock crowed, we beg Thee also to turn Thy Face towards those for whom we are a cock crow and grant them the grace of repentance.

Thursday Fourth Week in Lent

Dice/Lots

For Christ's own robes they cast the dice,
The Scriptures they fulfil;
The robe of grace is now the price
For which men gamble still.

O cast into God's hands your lot,
Regardless of the cost,
To win for those who have it not
This garment they have lost.

"They parted my garments amongst them; and upon my vesture they cast lots."
—Psalm 21:19

"The lot suppresseth contentions, and determineth even between the mighty."
—Proverbs 18:18

"And they said every one to his fellow: Come, and let us cast lots, that we may know why this evil is upon us. And they cast lots, and the lot fell upon Jonas."
—Jonas 1:7

"And after they had crucified him, they divided his garments, casting lots; that it might be fulfilled which was spoken by the prophet, saying: They divided my garments among them; and upon my vesture they cast lots."
—Matthew 27:35

"The soldiers therefore, when they had crucified him, took his garments, (and they made four parts, to every soldier a part,) and also his coat. Now the coat was without seam, woven from the top throughout. They said then one to another: Let us not cut it, but let us cast lots for it, whose it shall be; that the scripture might be fulfilled, saying: They have parted my garments among them, and upon my vesture they have cast lots. And the soldiers indeed did these things."
—John 19:23-24

"And they gave them lots, and the lot fell upon Matthias, and he was numbered with the eleven apostles."
—Acts of the Apostles 1:26

Meditation

Perhaps it may seem a small thing that lots were cast for the linen robe of Christ, yet no detail is recorded in Holy Scripture without reason. It was small in comparison to His other sufferings, yet it is great in the lessons it contains. In Biblical times, casting lots was a way of determining the will of God in a particular situation. We should also learn to seek the will of God whenever we are called upon to make decisions. Then, having done all we can in a given situation - all that is within our weak human power - we ought to put aside all worry and anxiety and, like those who cast the dice or drew lots, place our trust in Divine Providence.

By means of this instrument, Jesus was deprived of one of the barest necessities of life so that He might die completely poor. In our spiritual lives too, God sometimes deems it necessary for us to be deprived of that which seems most necessary to us in order that we might come to rely more fully on Him alone. The dice also teach us in imitation of Christ to bear patiently with small annoyances, trifling things to which we often pay too much attention.

To console Our Lord for those who deliberately put their eternal salvation in jeopardy, and to make reparation for sinful addictions such as gambling and excessive drinking, let us offer ourselves to Him as His dice to be treated however He pleases; and thus we shall help to win for needy souls the garment of grace.

Prayers

Eternal Father, I offer Thee all the sufferings of Jesus when the soldiers cast lots and divided His garments, in reparation for sinful addictions, especially gambling and drunkenness.

I cast my lot into Thy Hands, dear Lord, that Thou mayest use me as Thou wilt to win for souls the garment of grace.

Friday Fourth Week in Lent

Feast of the Precious Blood

Recall the drops of Blood He spilt
Upon the sinful earth;
Redeeming man, remitting guilt;
Each infinite in worth.

The angels gathered them with care;
We gather them up too,
To draw down graces everywhere
By offering them anew.

"Because the life of the flesh is in the blood: and I have given it to you, that you may make atonement with it upon the altar for your souls, and the blood may be for an expiation of the soul."

—Leviticus 17:11

"For this is my blood of the new testament, which shall be shed for many unto remission of sins."

—Matthew 26:28

"Knowing that you were not redeemed with corruptible things as gold or silver, . . . but with the precious blood of Christ, as of a lamb unspotted and undefiled."

—1 Peter 1:18-19

"For if the blood of goats and of oxen, and the ashes of an heifer being sprinkled, sanctify such as are defiled, to the cleansing of the flesh: how much more shall the blood of Christ, who by the Holy Ghost offered himself unspotted unto God, cleanse our conscience from dead works, to serve the living God?"

—Hebrews 9:13-14

"But now in Christ Jesus, you, who some time were afar off, are made nigh by the blood of Christ."

—Ephesians 2:13

"But if we walk in the light, as he also is in the light, we have fellowship one with another, and the blood of Jesus Christ his Son cleanseth us from all sin."

—1 John 1:7

"Blessed are they that wash their robes in the blood of the Lamb: that they may have a right to the tree of life, and may enter in by the gates into the city."

—Apocalypse 22:14

Meditation

As St. Thomas Aquinas mentions in the hymn, *Adoro Te Devote,* one single drop of the Precious Blood of Jesus would have amply sufficed to redeem the world. But Jesus loves us so greatly, that He shed for us every last drop of His Blood, and He continues to apply it to our souls through the Sacraments, especially the Sacrament of Penance. He gives us not only one chance to repent and be saved, but many. In shedding all of His Blood for us, Jesus wished to show us that we ought to love Him without measure in return.

"The angels… gathered up and preserved the smallest fragments of Our Lord's sacred Flesh which had been torn off by the frequent blows He received, as also the Blood with which the ground was sprinkled on those spots where He had fallen."[10] In imitation of the angels, and in the company of our Guardian Angel, let us hasten to gather up the drops of Precious Blood shed by Our Lord in His Passion and use them to purchase souls lest any be lost. The following ejaculations may be used frequently throughout the day for this intention.

[10] Dolorous Passion, by Anne Catherine Emmerich. Chap. LXII

Prayers

Eternal Father, I offer Thee the Precious Blood of Jesus to appease Thy justice and purchase souls.

My Jesus, pardon and mercy through the merits of Thy Precious Blood.

Precious Blood of Jesus, save us!

Saturday Fourth Week in Lent

Nails

Three nails bound Him to the tree,
But love transfixed Him more;
For there is scant fidelity
When love goes out the door.

Three kinds of vows need loyalty
To keep to what was spoken.
Preserve your own by charity;
Atone for pledges broken.

"For many dogs have encompassed me: the council of the malignant hath besieged me. They have dug my hands and feet."

—Psalm 21:17

"But he was wounded for our iniquities, he was bruised for our sins: the chastisement of our peace was upon him, and by his bruises we are healed."

—Isaias 53:5

"And when they were come to the place which is called Calvary, they crucified him there; and the robbers, one on the right hand, and the other on the left."

—Luke 23:33

"The other disciples therefore said to him: We have seen the Lord. But he said to them: Except I shall see in his hands the print of the nails, and put my finger into the place of the nails, and put my hand into his side, I will not believe."

—John 20:25

"For I, through the law, am dead to the law, that I may live to God: with Christ I am nailed to the cross."

—Galatians 2:19

Meditation

It was love more than iron nails which kept Jesus fastened to the cross. The three nails are symbolic of the three vows of religion and of all vows in general. It is only when love is lacking and where charity has grown cold that vows are likely to be broken. This is true of all vows, whether they be baptismal, matrimonial, religious, or other solemn promises made to God. Whatever our vocation and state in life may be, it is of the utmost importance to have charity – love of God and love of neighbour. To be lacking in this virtue and to deliberately efface it from one's life is to open the way for infidelity to one's vows.

As St. Therese discovered, and as every Christian must discover for themselves, love is the fulfilment of all vocations. Whatever our state in life may be, if we perform our duties with a pure intention of pleasing God and manifest our love by fidelity even in small things, we shall be imitating our Saviour Who laid down His life for His friends. Thus we shall indeed be worthy of the name Christian (little Christ) and we too shall have our share in the work of Redemption – and also in the reward.

Let us make reparation today for all those unfaithful to their vows, be they baptismal, matrimonial or religious vows. We can do this by greater fidelity to our duties and a more supernatural intention in performing them, whatever they may be.

Prayers

Eternal Father, I offer Thee the nails with which Jesus was crucified, the sufferings caused by them and the merits gained by them in reparation for all souls unfaithful to their vows.

O Jesus, grant us the grace, through the merits of Thy bitter passion, to be faithful to the vows that we have made.

Nails that pierced Jesus, nail me to the cross of Jesus, that I may live and die united to Jesus. [11]

[11] St. Alphonsus Liguori

Passion Sunday

Garments of Our Lord

His garments caused Our Lord much pain
When roughly torn away;
A source of grief they still remain
For Holy Church today.

Men treat Her with impunity,
Attacking as they please
Her seamless robe of unity—
Let us atone for these.

"They parted my garments amongst them; and upon my vesture they cast lots."

—Psalm 21:19

"And they shall strip thee of thy garments, and take away the instruments of thy glory."

—Ezechiel 23:26

"And after they had mocked him, they took off the cloak from him, and put on him his own garments, and led him away to crucify him."

—Matthew 27:31

"The soldiers therefore, when they had crucified him, took his garments, (and they made four parts, to every soldier a part,) and also his coat. Now the coat was without seam, woven from the top throughout. They said then one to another: Let us not cut it, but let us cast lots for it, whose it shall be; that the scripture might be fulfilled, saying: They have parted my garments among them, and upon my vesture they have cast lots. And the soldiers indeed did these things."

—John 19:23,24

Meditation

The garments of Our Lord were a source of great pain for Him in His Passion. Twice, at least, He was stripped of His garments; and they clung to His open wounds after the scourging. Once the blood had begun to dry, not even His Mother could have removed them without causing Him intense pain, but the soldiers did so very roughly, renewing the pain of all these wounds. And yet, the physical pain was small compared to the moral agony Jesus experienced in having His chaste body exposed to the gaze of the rude and scoffing crowd.

Jesus was also grieved when He saw the robe which His Blessed Mother had woven for Him torn apart by the soldiers, for He knew that this was but a reflection of how wicked men would divide the faithful and tear the very fabric of the Church and Her sacred doctrines through schism and heresies. The seamless robe was symbolic of the unity of the Church. However much She may be deprived of her external glory (represented by the divided garments) and however much it may be disputed, She will always remain one in Her truths, and in Her teachings. Even when She is seemingly given into the hands of Her enemies who would wish to tear Her to pieces, God will not permit Her unity to be destroyed. In Her sacred traditions and unchanging doctrines we find unity.

Prayers

Eternal Father, I offer Thee all the sufferings of Jesus in being stripped of His garments and in having them divided by the soldiers in reparation for those who seek to destroy the unity of the Church and for those who promote a false unity with Her enemies.

My Jesus, I beg Thee to unite Thy scattered flock under a truly holy Pope. May the restoration of Thy Church come soon!

Monday in Passion Week

Eclipse of the Sun

The sun's eclipse, the loss of light,
Betokens desolation;
For Jesus' Soul was in dark night,
Deprived of consolation.

Let us accept our tiny share
In this, Christ's greatest trial;
For those in darkness everywhere,
That grace on them may smile.

"And my soul is troubled exceedingly: but thou, O Lord, how long? Turn to me, O Lord, and deliver my soul: O save me for thy mercy's sake."
—Psalm 6:4-5

"For my soul is filled with evils: and my life hath drawn nigh to hell. I am counted among them that go down to the pit: I am become as a man without help... All the day I cried to thee, O Lord: I stretched out my hands to thee... Lord, why castest thou off my prayer: why turnest thou away thy face from me?"
—Psalms 87:4-5,10,15

"Then he saith to them: My soul is sorrowful even unto death: stay you here, and watch with me."
—Matthew 26:38

"And when the sixth hour was come, there was darkness over the whole earth until the ninth hour. And at the ninth hour, Jesus cried out with a loud voice, saying: Eloi, Eloi, lamma sabacthani? Which is, being interpreted, My God, my God, why hast thou forsaken me?"
—Mark 15:33-34

"And it was almost the sixth hour; and there was darkness over all the earth until the ninth hour. And the sun was darkened, and the veil of the temple was rent in the midst. And Jesus crying out with a loud voice, said: Father, into thy hands I commend my spirit. And saying this, he gave up the ghost."
—Luke 23:44-46

Meditation

While many people contemplate the physical sufferings of Jesus in His Passion, there are very few who consider the sufferings of His Soul. The sun's eclipse caused darkness over the whole land and this was a figure of the Soul of Jesus enveloped in the most painful spiritual darkness. Between the radiant light of heavenly glory and our guilty earth came the dark and oppressing burden of sin which blotted out from Our Lord in His Sacred Humanity every last bit of consolation. By considering this, we may draw courage and strength to bear our own spiritual trials, such as dryness and distractions in prayer, not merely with resignation, but willingly, so that we may bring Him some consolation and make reparation for souls in the darkness of sin and error. Our willing acceptance of interior trials will also benefit those who are suffering in similar ways, and obtain for them the courage they need to persevere.

Prayers

Eternal Father, I offer Thee the spiritual darkness endured by Thy Son and by many faithful souls in reparation for those who prefer the darkness of sin and error to the light of grace and truth.

O Jesus, to console Thee for the sufferings of Thy most holy Soul, especially in the darkness which enveloped Thee during Thy bitter Passion, I offer Thee all the sufferings of my own soul.

Tuesday in Passion Week

Water, Sponges, Cloths

The sponge and water which did rinse
The blood from corpse and hair
Were used as loving instruments,
Man's insults to repair.

The water of repentant tears,
Fidelity to grace,
And daily duties done with care,
Shall comfort Christ's Sweet Face.

"And when it was evening, there came a certain rich man of Arimathea, named Joseph, who also himself was a disciple of Jesus. He went to Pilate, and asked the body of Jesus. Then Pilate commanded that the body should be delivered And Joseph taking the body, wrapped it up in a clean linen cloth."
—Matthew 27:57-59

"And Joseph buying fine linen, and taking him down, wrapped him up in the fine linen, and laid him in a sepulchre which was hewed out of a rock. And he rolled a stone to the door of the sepulchre."
—Mark 15:46

"This man went to Pilate, and begged the body of Jesus And taking him down, he wrapped him in fine linen, and laid him in a sepulchre that was hewed in stone, wherein never yet any man had been laid."
—Luke 23:52-53

"And Nicodemus also came, (he who at the first came to Jesus by night,) bringing a mixture of myrrh and aloes, about an hundred pound weight. They took therefore the body of Jesus, and bound it in linen cloths, with the spices, as the manner of the Jews is to bury."
—John 19:39-40

Meditation

The Evangelists do not expressly state, but we may take it for granted, that the Body of Our Lord was lovingly and reverently washed before being wrapped in the linen cloths and placed in the tomb. It must have brought Jesus much consolation to have His Sacred Body tended to by loving hands, just as He is consoled each time when He is worthily received in Holy Communion. Today let us employ the instruments used to prepare His Body for burial as a means of making reparation, especially to His Holy Face, which was the object of Mary's special care and attention.

The water is symbolic of tears of compunction (or at least the desire for them) which have their source in true repentance for our sins. The sponges represent fidelity to grace and to the inspirations of the Holy Ghost. Just as sponges readily absorb water, so we must be docile to the inward promptings of our conscience and repent of our infidelities in this regard. The cloths make us appreciate and value careful performance of our daily duties. However mundane and tiresome they may be, a pure intention of pleasing God will give them great value in His sight.

Prayers

Eternal Father, receive the reparation we offer this day to the Holy Face of Thy Beloved Son, and for His sake, have mercy on Thy guilty creatures.

My Jesus, I offer Thee all the instruments lovingly used to prepare Thy Sacred Body for burial and all my prayers and good works of this day to console Thy Sacred Face for all the injuries and insults of wicked men which have cruelly disfigured It.

Wednesday in Passion Week

Stone

The stone they used to seal the tomb
Recalls each hardened heart,
And multitudes of men from whom
God's grace is kept apart.

By casting all our care on Christ,
From His own strength we borrow;
And beg that souls may be enticed
To share Our Lady's sorrow.

"Cast thy care upon the Lord, and he shall sustain thee: he shall not suffer the just to waver for ever."
—Psalm 54:23

"And I will give you a new heart, and put a new spirit within you: and I will take away the stony heart out of your flesh, and will give you a heart of flesh. And I will put my spirit in the midst of you: and I will cause you to walk in my commandments, and to keep my judgments, and do them."
—Ezechiel 36:26-27

"Jesus saith to them: Have you never read in the Scriptures: The stone which the builders rejected, the same is become the head of the corner? By the Lord this has been done; and it is wonderful in our eyes."
—Matthew 21:42

"And they departing, made the sepulchre sure, sealing the stone, and setting guards."
—Matthew 27:66

"And all drank the same spiritual drink; (and they drank of the spiritual rock that followed them, and the rock was Christ.)"
—1 Corinthians 10:4

Meditation

Today let us contemplate the stone which sealed the entrance to the sepulchre, and the sorrow of Mary when it was rolled into place, separating her from the Body of Jesus. Only those who know what it is to lose a loved one or to be deprived of the sensible presence of God can begin to appreciate the grief of the Immaculate Mother.

Our soul is like the tomb where the Body of Jesus rests, even if He is silent. St Paul tells us that 'the rock was Christ.' We must give Jesus Christ His rightful place in our life, being docile to His will so that He Himself will guard the entrance of our soul and prevent anything from entering in which is unworthy of His presence.

A rock can be cold or warm as can our feelings towards God. This does not alter its strength. Feelings do not matter much in the spiritual life. What is important is the dedication of our will to the service of God. True love can exist, independently of emotion. It is shown by one's readiness to do anything to please the Beloved. The Spiritual Rock, however, can never change; It is always solid and can be depended on to bear our weight. We must cast our care upon Him and He will support us with His unfailing strength. Let us endeavour to spend this day in filial dependence upon God and fidelity to His will in all things. This will be a fitting reparation for those whose hearts are hardened to His grace.

Prayers

Eternal Father, I offer Thee all the sufferings of Mary when the stone separated her from the Body of Jesus, in reparation for those whose hearts are hardened to grace. May her sorrowful tears and the Precious Blood of Jesus soften such hearts of stone and bring them to repentance.

Thou art my strength O Lord; in Thee have I trusted; let me not be confounded.

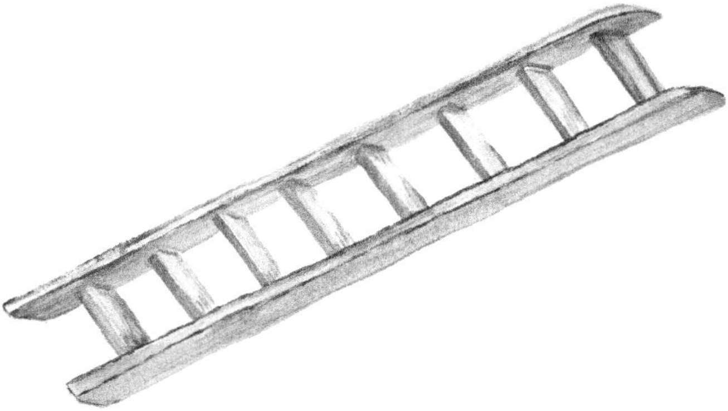

Thursday in Passion Week

Ladder

The ladder used by Jesus' friends
To take Him from the tree,
Recalls the way He still descends
At Mass - our Calvary.

Our mediator is the priest,
A bridge 'twixt God and man.
We pray for priests whose lives have ceased
To be the best they can.

“And he saw in his sleep a ladder standing upon the earth, and the top thereof touching heaven: the angels also of God ascending and descending by it.”
—Genesis 28:12

“And Joseph buying fine linen, and taking him down, wrapped him up in the fine linen, and laid him in a sepulchre which was hewed out of a rock. And he rolled a stone to the door of the sepulchre.”
—Mark 15:46

“And taking him down, he wrapped him in fine linen, and laid him in a sepulchre that was hewed in stone, wherein never yet any man had been laid.”
—Luke 23:53

“And after these things, Joseph of Arimathea (because he was a disciple of Jesus, but secretly for fear of the Jews) besought Pilate that he might take away the body of Jesus. And Pilate gave leave. He came therefore, and took the body of Jesus.”
—John 19:38

“For there is one God, and one mediator of God and men, the man Christ Jesus.”
—1 Timothy 2:5

Meditation

The ladder was used by Joseph of Arimathea and Nicodemus to take the Body of Christ down from the cross. In performing this loving service, they resemble our priests who bring down from Heaven the Body and Blood of Jesus. Like the angels in Jacob's dream, the priest must also act as a mediator between God and man. A priest, more than anyone else, must closely resemble Our Lord Jesus Christ, who is both God and Man. The priest is human like ourselves, and yet when he ascends the altar, hears confessions or administers the sacraments, he is acting in the Person of Christ. His humanity keeps him among us; his likeness to Christ raises him up to God, so that a faithful priest is truly like an angel ascending and descending the ladder with which Jesus Christ has bridged the chasm between God and man.

Thursday has long been dedicated to the Mystery of the Holy Eucharist. It was on Holy Thursday that Our Lord instituted this most Blessed Sacrament and also the Catholic priesthood. Let us therefore make reparation today for unfaithful priests, and implore special graces for them all, both faithful and unfaithful, that they may live in a manner worthy of their Divine vocation.

Prayers

Eternal Father, may all the honour shown to the Body of Jesus when He was taken down from the cross, continue to be rendered by all who receive that Sacred Body, and especially by Thy priests at whose word He descends upon our altars.

O Lord, grant us many holy priests!

Friday in Passion Week

Feast of the Sorrowful Mother

Recall the grief which pierced the soul
Of Mary and her Son;
The pain of each made one great whole—
It mingled into one.

O Mary, grant that we may share
Thy sympathy, like John;
Consoling Jesus everywhere
His Passion carries on.

"Thou seest it, for thou considerest labour and sorrow: that thou mayst deliver them into thy hands. To thee is the poor man left: thou wilt be a helper to the orphan."

—Psalm 9/10:14

"For the affliction of the daughter of my people I am afflicted, and made sorrowful, astonishment hath taken hold on me. Is there no balm in Galaad? or is no physician there? Why then is not the wound of the daughter of my people closed?"

—Jeremias 8:21-22

"O all ye that pass by the way, attend, and see if there be any sorrow like to my sorrow: for he hath made a vintage of me, as the Lord spoke in the day of his fierce anger."

—Lamentations 1:12

"Behold, O Lord, for I am in distress, my bowels are troubled: my heart is turned within me, for I am full of bitterness: abroad the sword destroyeth, and at home there is death alike. They have heard that I sigh, and there is none to comfort me: all my enemies have heard of my evil, they have rejoiced that thou hast done it: thou hast brought a day of consolation, and they shall be like unto me. Let all their evil be present before thee: and make vintage of them, as thou hast made vintage of me for all my iniquities: for my sighs are many, and my heart is sorrowful."

—Lamentations 1:20-22

Meditation

Among the many instruments used in the Passion of Our Divine Redeemer, we cannot overlook the suffering Our Lord experienced on seeing His sorrowful and Immaculate Mother on His journey to Calvary and at the foot of the cross. Apart from the inward desolation and sense of abandonment by His Eternal Father, there was no greater suffering Jesus experienced than witnessing the sufferings of His Mother. The more two hearts love each other, the more each shares by compassion in the sufferings of the other. In no case was this more true than with Jesus and Mary.

The suffering Jesus experienced in His Physical Body and Immortal Soul, was likewise experienced by His Blessed Mother in her Immaculate Heart. The more she loved Him, the more she suffered, and the more she suffered, the more it increased the sufferings of Jesus. From the height of the cross Jesus looked into an Immaculate Mirror in the person of His Blessed Mother, and saw there a perfect reflection of His dolorous suffering.

Let us implore of these two Sorrowful Hearts the grace to love them greatly in return for all they suffered for us; a love which will move us to compassionate the Catholic Church, the Mystical Body of Christ, in which the sufferings of the Passion are being renewed in a particular manner at the present time.

Prayers

Jesus, Mary, I love Thee; save souls!

Sorrowful and Immaculate Heart of Mary, pray for us who have recourse to Thee.

Saturday in Passion Week

Pliers

The pliers serve as illustration
Of how we ought to spend
Our lives in making reparation,
Christ's Body to defend.

They pulled the nails from Hands and Feet,
Tugged thorns from Sacred Brow;
And we this work of love complete
By prayer and penance now.

"… he hath been zealous for his God, and hath made atonement for the wickedness of the children of Israel."

—Numbers 25:13

"And David said to God: I have sinned exceedingly in doing this: I beseech thee take away the iniquity of thy servant, for I have done foolishly."

—1 Paralipomenon 21:8

"As far as the east is from the west, so far hath he removed our iniquities from us."

—Psalm 102:12

"Thus saith the Lord God: Remove the diadem, take off the crown: is it not this that hath exalted the low one, and brought down him that was high."

—Ezechiel 21:26

"And when they had fulfilled all things that were written of him, taking him down from the tree, they laid him in a sepulchre."

—Acts of the Apostles 13:29

Meditation

At La Salette Our Lady appeared wearing a Crucifix around her neck which had a pair of pliers and a hammer fixed to the horizontal beam of the cross. This was symbolic of the message she brought, which was a most grave one; for she spoke of the horrible effects of sin, the extent to which it was spreading and the urgent need for reparation to hold back the arm of Divine Justice. These are her own words which we would do well to ponder today: *"The sins of those dedicated to God cry out towards Heaven and call for vengeance, and now vengeance is at their door, for there is no one left to beg mercy and forgiveness for the people. There are no more generous souls, there is no one left worthy of offering a spotless sacrifice to the Eternal for the sake of the world."*

The hammer symbolises the work of sin, for it was used to inflict pain. The pliers are symbolic of the work of reparation since they were not used to inflict pain but to remove the cause of it; namely, the nails and the thorns. To make reparation is to withdraw the nails and thorns of sin from the wounded members of the Mystical Body of Christ, using the pliers of prayer and sacrifice, held firmly in the grip of love. We need not invent new and terrible penances for ourselves. It would be imprudent to do so without a special inspiration from God. It will be quite sufficient if we succeed in using every opportunity for sacrifice which presents itself to us in the course of the day. The greater our love for God, the more we shall notice and make use of such opportunities. The smaller they seem, the less danger there is of losing the value of them through pride. As St. Augustine observes, little things are indeed little, but to be faithful in little things is a great thing. May this be our focus today!

Prayers

Eternal Father, I offer Thee the pliers used to remove the nails and thorns from the Body of Jesus and all loving efforts to make reparation in atonement for all those sins which caused Our Lady to weep at La Salette.

O Jesus, help me to be faithful in little things that I may thereby help to remove from Thy Mystical Body the nails and thorns of sin.

Sunday in Holy Week (Palm Sunday)

Inscription

They hung a title on the tree
For passers-by to read;
They called Him king in mockery,
Though He is King indeed.

Let us atone for false disguise
Where pious looks mask blame,
While taking care lest we likewise
Should mock His Kingly Name.

"And they put over his head his cause written: THIS IS JESUS THE KING OF THE JEWS."
—Matthew 27:37

"And the inscription of his cause was written over: THE KING OF THE JEWS."
—Mark 15:26

"Blessed be the king who cometh in the name of the Lord, peace in heaven, and glory on high."
—Luke 19:38

"And Pilate wrote a title also, and he put it upon the cross. And the writing was: JESUS OF NAZARETH, THE KING OF THE JEWS. This title therefore many of the Jews did read: because the place where Jesus was crucified was nigh to the city: and it was written in Hebrew, in Greek, and in Latin."
—John 19:19-20

"Blotting out the handwriting of the decree that was against us, which was contrary to us. And he hath taken the same out of the way, fastening it to the cross and despoiling the principalities and powers, he hath exposed them confidently in open shew, triumphing over them in himself."
—Colossians 2:14-15

Meditation

On Palm Sunday we recall how Jesus entered Jerusalem in triumph, hailed by the people as King. Yet only a few days later, the very same people cried out against Him, demanding that He be crucified. On Good Friday, even while condemning Him to death, Pontius Pilate proclaimed Jesus to be a King by causing this inscription to be placed over His Head: JESUS OF NAZARETH, KING OF THE JEWS.

Today there are many who refuse to acknowledge Christ's Kingship. Others proclaim it in word, but in practice they deny it. There are also some who serve Him in appearance, but they turn into mockery the outward homage they offer Him by the inward dispositions of their hearts. Those who serve Him best are those whose attitude towards Him is motivated by love and whose outward conduct is a true reflection of their hearts. Jesus is indeed a King and He has the right to do with us as He wishes, for He has redeemed us. Nevertheless, He respects our free will and only exercises His full rights over us whenever and wherever He is invited to do so. Let us reproach ourselves for our own infidelity towards Christ the King, and beg Him to establish anew His reign in our hearts. Nothing else will bring true peace to our souls, for He is the Prince of Peace. An earnest endeavour to render Him homage by docility to His will shall be our means of making reparation for bad rulers, for those guilty of hypocrisy, and for all those who oppose His reign.

Prayers

Eternal Father, I offer Thee all the sincere homage offered to Thy Son in reparation for bad rulers, hypocrites, and all those opposed to His universal Kingship.

Hail, my Jesus and my King! I offer Thee my homage, not in mockery but with all the ardour and love of which my poor heart is capable.

Monday in Holy Week

Wormwood and Gall

The wormwood and the bitter gall
Were offered to kill pain.
He tasted, but would not drink all—
His virtue is our gain.

He shows us how to mortify
Ourselves, as He has done;
And by our penance to supply
For sinners who do none.

"And they gave me gall for my food, and in my thirst they gave me vinegar to drink."

—Psalms 68:22

"But they have gone after the perverseness of their own heart, and after Baalim, which their fathers taught them. Therefore thus saith the Lord of hosts the God of Israel: Behold I will feed this people with wormwood, and give them water of gall to drink."

—Jeremias 9:14-15

"He hath filled me with bitterness, he hath inebriated me with wormwood. Remember my poverty, and transgression, the wormwood, and the gall."

—Lamentations 3:15,19

"And they gave him wine to drink mingled with gall. And when he had tasted, he would not drink."

—Matthew 27:34

"And the name of the star is called Wormwood. And the third part of the waters became wormwood; and many men died of the waters, because they were made bitter."

—Apocalypse 8:11

Meditation

Because the bitter cup of His approaching Passion must never have been far from the thoughts of Our Lord during this week, we meditate today on the wormwood and gall. These bitter herbs mingled with wine helped to deaden the pain and were offered to those condemned to be crucified as an act of charity by pious women. Jesus tasted this beverage to show His appreciation, but in a spirit of mortification He did not take it all, leaving us an example of the spirit of sacrifice which ought to mark His followers. This was a voluntary mortification. He tasted the bitterness without experiencing the pain-killing effects of this beverage. When we consider how extremely thirsty Jesus was, and how immense His sufferings were, it was a truly heroic sacrifice, and so it teaches us how there can be great merit in sacrifices which appear small and insignificant.

As Lent is drawing to its close, let us make a greater effort to end it well in a spirit of mortification and in reparation for those who have neglected to do penance. Our Lord warns us that unless we do penance, we shall all likewise perish. Our voluntary penances may merit the grace of repentance for those who neglect this important duty, and if we unite them to the sufferings Our Lord endured in tasting the bitter gall, they will be easier to bear.

Prayers

Eternal Father, I offer Thee all the sufferings of Jesus in tasting the wormwood and the gall, together with the voluntary mortifications performed this Lent; in reparation for all those who neglect to do penance, especially during this Holy Season.

O Jesus, may Thy bitterness be turned to sweetness and Thy sorrow into joy at the sight of those whom Thou hast saved by Thy Passion and Death.

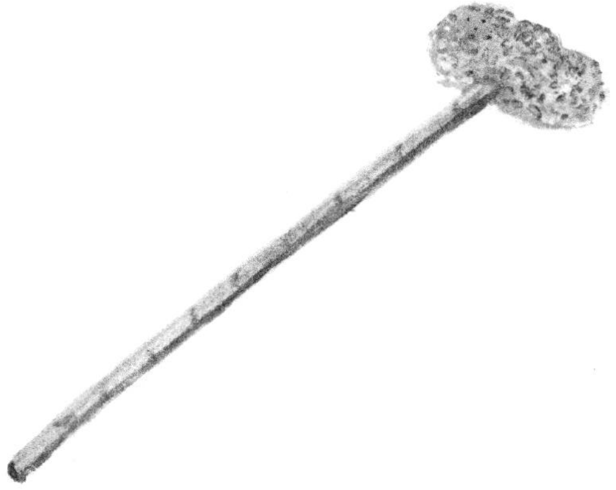

Tuesday in Holy Week

Sponge on a Reed of Hyssop

The brutal soldiers laughed and joked;
Christ's plea they feigned to heed.
A sponge in vinegar they soaked,
And held up on a reed.

They used it to increase His pain,
But we give what He asks;
Atoning for the proud and vain
By humble daily tasks.

"In thy sight are all they that afflict me; my heart hath expected reproach and misery. And I looked for one that would grieve together with me, but there was none: and for one that would comfort me, and I found none. And they gave me gall for my food, and in my thirst they gave me vinegar to drink."

—Psalm 68:21-22

"And immediately one of them running took a sponge, and filled it with vinegar; and put it on a reed, and gave him to drink."

—Matthew 27:48

"And one running and filling a sponge with vinegar, and putting it upon a reed, gave him to drink, saying: Stay, let us see if Elias come to take him down."

—Mark 15:36

"And the soldiers also mocked him, coming to him, and offering him vinegar."

—Luke 23:36

"Now there was a vessel set there full of vinegar. And they, putting a sponge full of vinegar about hyssop, put it to his mouth."

—John 19:29

Meditation

Tuesday is the day of the week especially dedicated to the Holy Face. As the instrument for today we shall take the sponge stuck on a reed of hyssop. When the soldier held it up to Our Lord's parched lips, dripping with vinegar, we can imagine it must have stung the wounds of His Holy Face very much. Instead of mocking Jesus and increasing His sufferings, we can use the sponge in loving reparation. We will fill it with the water He craves when we devote ourselves to our daily duties; and perform some extra little charitable services for others with a pure intention of pleasing Him. This will console Him in His thirst and soothe the wounds of His Holy Face.

Like the reed, we are also weak and frail creatures, but God wills to use us, nevertheless, to make reparation. We must be docile instruments in His hands, so that we may be filled with His strength; and we must cling faithfully to the common sponge – the holiness which is within reach of everyone by loving and careful performance of daily duties.

Since the sponge also reminds us of those who pamper the body to the detriment of the soul, let us make reparation today for sins of pride, vanity and self-indulgence.

Prayers

Eternal Father, I wish to perform all my duties today in a spirit of loving reparation to the Holy Face of Jesus and to atone for all those who pamper their body while neglecting to care for their soul.

O Jesus, like a frail reed, I wish to hold up a sponge of consolation to Thy Holy Face by the careful and loving performance of my duties. Be Thou my strength, O Lord, and help me to carry out my resolve.

Wednesday in Holy Week

Kiss of Judas

Our Saviour could not be deceived
By Judas and his kiss.
By treachery His Heart was grieved—
He often spoke of this.

The Church has been betrayed likewise
By clergymen who pose
As friends, though traitors in disguise;
Let us atone for those.

"For if my enemy had reviled me, I would verily have borne with it. And if he that hated me had spoken great things against me, I would perhaps have hidden myself from him. But thou a man of one mind, my guide, and my familiar, Who didst take sweetmeats together with me: in the house of God we walked with consent."

—Psalm 54:13-15

"And he that betrayed him, gave them a sign, saying: Whomsoever I shall kiss, that is he, hold him fast. And forthwith coming to Jesus, he said: Hail, Rabbi. And he kissed him."

—Matthew 26:48-49

"And he that betrayed him, had given them a sign, saying: Whomsoever I shall kiss, that is he; lay hold on him, and lead him away carefully. And when he was come, immediately going up to him, he saith: Hail, Rabbi; and he kissed him."

—Mark 14:44-45

"As he was yet speaking, behold a multitude; and he that was called Judas, one of the twelve, went before them, and drew near to Jesus, for to kiss him. And Jesus said to him: Judas, dost thou betray the Son of man with a kiss?"

—Luke 22:47-48

Meditation

Wednesday of Holy Week marks the sad anniversary of the betrayal of Our Lord by Judas, for it was on this day that he resolved to commit this crime, fixed upon the price of thirty silver coins in exchange for his wicked deed, and agreed upon his treacherous kiss as a sign. And therefore it was also on this day that he incurred the guilt of what he actually accomplished on the following night. Since the Evangelists all mention the betrayal of Judas several times and Our Lord Himself spoke of it so much, we may conclude that it was one of His greatest sorrows that He should be betrayed by one of His own. If we have ever been let down by someone we loved dearly and trusted deeply, then we may have a faint idea of the sorrow it brought the loving Heart of our Saviour to receive the kiss of the traitor as a recompense for all the trust and love He had shown him in making him an Apostle.

We cannot help thinking of another betrayal which has taken place – namely that of the Mystical Body of Christ which has been delivered into the hands of Her enemies by disloyal children, particularly those among the ranks of the clergy who have let themselves be bribed by money, honour and power. Let us therefore make reparation today for all those who appear outwardly to be the Church's friends but who have in reality betrayed Her, begging pardon and mercy for them while we strive to forgive those who have forsaken us in our time of need.

Prayers

Eternal Father, I offer Thee the sufferings of Jesus in receiving the kiss of Judas in reparation for those who have likewise betrayed the Church into the hands of Her enemies.

O Jesus, to console Thee for the kiss of Judas, I venerate Thy Holy Face with a loving kiss and with all the sincerity of my heart.

Holy Thursday

The Towel

The towel they used removed no guilt
From Pilate and the Traitor.
Though both the Blood of Jesus spilt,
The latter's sin was greater.

How many souls repeat this act
By badly made confessions!
Yet true contrition may, in fact,
Atone for such transgressions.

"Have mercy on me, O God, according to thy great mercy. And according to the multitude of thy tender mercies blot out my iniquity. Wash me yet more from my iniquity, and cleanse me from my sin."
—Psalm 50:3-4

"And Pilate seeing that he prevailed nothing, but that rather a tumult was made; taking water washed his hands before the people, saying: I am innocent of the blood of this just man; look you to it."
—Matthew 27:24

"He riseth from supper, and layeth aside his garments, and having taken a towel, girded himself. After that, he putteth water into a basin, and began to wash the feet of the disciples, and to wipe them with the towel wherewith he was girded… Simon Peter saith to him: Lord, not only my feet, but also my hands and my head. Jesus saith to him: He that is washed, needeth not but to wash his feet, but is clean wholly. And you are clean, but not all. For he knew who he was that would betray him; therefore he said: You are not all clean."
—John 13:4-5,9-11

"Jesus answered: Thou shouldst not have any power against me, unless it were given thee from above. Therefore, he that hath delivered me to thee, hath the greater sin."
—John 19:11

Meditation

The towel used by Pilate to dry his hands after he had washed them in front of the people, reminds us also of the towel used by Jesus while washing the feet of His disciples at the Last Supper. Both for Judas and for Pilate, the towel signified a hypocritical attempt to have the guilt of their crimes washed away, since they lacked true contrition for the evil they had done by delivering Jesus into the hands of His enemies. Since then, how many times this hypocrisy has been repeated! Bad and sacrilegious confessions made without true contrition and without any intention of amending one's life, repeat the actions of Judas and of Pilate. To make such a vain pretence of repentance is to make a mockery of the Sacrament of Penance. It is like spitting in the Face of Jesus. Let us cultivate true contrition for our own sins and endeavour to make a profitable use of the Sacrament of Penance when we can. We shall thus offer Jesus a towel with which to wipe His Holy Face, making reparation for those who repeat the betrayal of Judas and the hypocrisy of Pilate through bad confessions.

Prayers

Eternal Father, in reparation for sacrilegious confessions which repeat the actions of Judas and of Pilate, grant that I may have true contrition for my own sins and thus offer Jesus a towel with which to wipe His Holy Face.

Sweet Jesus, may the true contrition and good confessions of Thy faithful console Thee, and be like a towel to wipe away the sins of those who spit in Thy Face by bad confessions.

Good Friday

The Footrest

The footrest fastened to the tree
Prolonged a painful death,
Renewing Jesus' agony
Each time He gasped for breath.

Contritely let us beg for grace
To be more mortified;
And let our feet the steps retrace
Of Jesus Crucified.

“Exalt ye the Lord our God, and adore his footstool, for it is holy.”

—Psalm 98:5

“The Lord said to my Lord: Sit thou at my right hand: Until I make thy enemies thy footstool. The Lord will send forth the sceptre of thy power out of Sion: rule thou in the midst of thy enemies.”

—Psalm 109:1-2

“We will go into his tabernacle: We will adore in the place where his feet stood.”

—Psalm 131:7

“And David himself saith in the book of Psalms: The Lord said to my Lord, sit thou on my right hand till I make thy enemies thy footstool.”

—Luke 20:42-43

“But this man offering one sacrifice for sins, for ever sitteth on the right hand of God, From henceforth expecting, until his enemies be made his footstool.”

—Hebrews 10:13

Meditation

The footrest was fastened to the cross beneath the feet of a crucified victim, not as an act of mercy, but to prolong their suffering by providing them with a means to prevent themselves being strangled immediately. The position of Our Lord on the cross with His arms stretched as far as possible meant that He had to raise Himself by pushing Himself up using the footrest very time He took a breath. This was a great torture especially because of the nails piercing His feet.

Taking the footrest as today's instrument let us recall how our own feet have led us on paths of sin when we failed to submit humbly to the reign of Jesus in our souls. We remember also how we ourselves have contributed to the Passion of Our Saviour, making reparation for our own sins and the sins which we have led others to commit. We can do this by striving to accept our daily crosses in a spirit of mortification, and by adding our own voluntary acts of self-denial to them in order to become a more faithful disciple of Jesus Crucified.

At present the just are afflicted by the wicked, but at the end of time, all the enemies of God will be cast down under His feet and He will make them His footstool. How miserable we shall be if that is our lot and if we will never be granted to behold His Face! We do not know how much time remains to us. It is important that we use it well, for the final sentence of the Just Judge will be eternal and unchanging.

Prayers

Eternal Father, I offer Thee all the sufferings of Jesus when His feet were nailed to the footrest in reparation for my own sins and for all the sins which I have led others to commit.

Most loving Jesus, my Crucified Saviour, I beg Thee to grant me a true spirit of mortification and to make me Thy faithful disciple. As I go about my daily duties today, I wish to remain in spirit at Thy feet with Mary, weeping in contrition for my sins.

Lord Jesus Crucified, have mercy on me, a sinner.

Holy Saturday

The Seal

The tomb was closely watched and sealed
By truth-denying men;
Yet Truth cannot remain concealed;
And Jesus rose again

May we, who have been sealed and signed
By sanctifying grace,
Bring Jesus Christ to all mankind
Through likeness to His Face.

"And the Lord said to him: Go through the midst of the city, through the midst of Jerusalem: and mark Thau[12] upon the foreheads of the men that sigh, and mourn for all the abominations that are committed in the midst thereof."

—Ezechiel 9:4

"And they departing, made the sepulchre sure, sealing the stone, and setting guards."

—Matthew 27:66

"And they sung a new canticle, saying: Thou art worthy, O Lord, to take the book, and to open the seals thereof; because thou wast slain, and hast redeemed us to God, in thy blood, out of every tribe, and tongue, and people, and nation."

—Apoc. 5:9

"And I saw another angel ascending from the rising of the sun, having the sign of the living God; and he cried with a loud voice to the four angels, to whom it was given to hurt the earth and the sea, saying: Hurt not the earth, nor the sea, nor the trees, till we sign the servants of our God in their foreheads."

—Apocalypse 7:2-3

[12] See note on page 58

Meditation

The seal was very fittingly the final instrument used to complete the Lord's Passion and burial. The Pharisees thought that by sealing the tomb, this would be the end of Jesus and His miracles. In reality it was only the beginning. No seal or power of any earthly ruler was able to prevent the Resurrection of Jesus Christ and neither can it destroy His Mystical Body, the Church, through whom He continues His life on earth.

As it was by dying for our sakes that the Lamb opened the seven seals of the book of life, so also it is by dying to the world and to ourselves that we shall find true life. The sign of the Cross is the sign with which we have been sealed to show that we are truly followers of Christ. Let us therefore take up our cross with courage and follow in the footsteps of the Lamb who was slain, so that we may be found worthy to have our names written in the book of life

Prayers

Eternal Father, I beg Thee to imprint upon the hearts of many souls the most precious seal of the Holy Face of Jesus, that Thou mayest restore in them Thy own image and likeness which they have disfigured by sin.

O Jesus, through the merits of Thy Passion and Death by which Thou didst open the Seven Seals of the book of life, I beg Thee to seal me with the sign of Thy cross and to inscribe my name in the book of life, never to be blotted out.

Dear Christian soul, now Lent is done,
Strive that you may retain
The virtues gained, the merits won,
Lest it have passed in vain.

So frequently throughout the year,
Take up this book again,
And use the Arma found in here
To fight as valiant men.

Appendix

A Fifteenth Century Poem

We are indebted to a student of Oxford University (who wishes to remain anonymous) for kindly translating the Middle English manuscript of the following poem into modern English.

O Vernicle

from BL Additional MS 22029

Verse 1: Vernicle [Veil of Veronica]

Thee vernicle, I honour Him and thee,
That He made through His secrecy.
The cloth he set over His face,
The imprint he left there of His grace.
His mouth, His nose, His eyes two,
His beard, His hair He did also.
Shield me Lord, because in my life,
I have sinned with my senses five,
Namely, with a mouth of slandering,
Of false oaths and backbiting,
And also making boast by tongue,
Of the many sins that I have done.
Lord of Heaven, forgive it me,
By virtue of the face that I here see.

Verse 2: Knife of Circumcision

This knife betokens the circumcision,
That destroyed our sins, each one and the sum,
Of our first father Adam,
Through whom we took the nature of man.
From the temptation of lechery,
Lord keep me until I die.

Verse 3: Pelican

The pelican his blood does bleed,
With that (blood) his chicks to feed. It betokens that upon the rood,
Our Lord fed us with His precious blood,
When He bought us out of Hell,
In love and bliss with Him to dwell,
And to be our Father and our food,
And we His children, meek and good.

Verse 4: Thirty Pennies

Also the pennies of which Judas counted/told,
(The reason) why Jesus Christ was sold.
Lord shield me from treason and avarice,
That therein I (in) no way decease.

Verse 5: Lantern

The lantern inside which they carried the light,
When Christ was taken within the night.
Lord keep me from the night-time's sin,
That I never be taken therein.

Verse 6: Swords and Clubs

The swords and staves that they bear,
There Jesus Christ to terrify with there.
From fiends Lord, preserve me,
Lord, that I of fiends fearless be.

Verse 7: Rod

With a rod He suffered a stroke,
With it the Jews His head they broke.
With a cheerful face and a mild mind,
He endured it all and still He stood.

When I do wrong or any man wrong me,
May it be forgiven for that pity.

Verse 8: Hands

The hands, Lord, that tore off your hair,
And the hand that smacked thee under the ear.
For that pain Lord, be my succour there,
That I have sinned with pride of hair,
And all other sins also,
That with ears I have listened to.

Verse 9: Blindfold

The cloth in front of your eyes two,
To strike thee they bound it so.
Lord, keep me from vengeance,
Of immaturity and of ignorance,
And further sins also,
That I have seen with my eyes two,
And with my nose smelled also,
Both old and ill.

Verse 10: Garments

Your own garment that had seams none,
The purple (cloth) that they cast lots upon,
Lord, be my succour and my help,
(When) that my body has used clothing amiss.

Verse 11: Scourges

With great sticks you were completely dashed,
With sharp scourges utterly lashed.
Lord, succour me from these sins,
Of sloth and also of idleness.

Verse 12: Crown of Thorns

The crown of thorns on your head pressed,
Your hair to tear, your skin to pierce.
Lord, succour me from these sins,
Of sloth and also of idleness.

Verse 13: Column of Scourging

To the pillar Lord also,
With a rope men bound thee too.
Hard drawn and strained tightly,
The sinews from the bonds burst.
Lord, loose me from bonds in distress,
Though I did unkind against kindness.

Verse 14: Bleeding Footprints

You bore the cross over the lake,
Out of Jerusalem at the gate.
Your footsteps sweet and good,
Were seen through the shedding of your precious blood.
You met with the women of Bethlehem,
And also the women of Jerusalem.
They all wept for your torment.
To them you said openly,
"Weep not for my woe,
But for your children also.
For them you may sorely weep,
And salt tears for them leak.
For they shall have torment hard,
For a hundred winters hereafterward.
Your steps of grace for us give pardon,
When we go with devotion
On pilgrimage on horse or on foot.
Of my sins Lord, be my remedy.

Verse 15: Nails

The nails through feet and hands also Lord, keep me out of sin and woe, That I in my life have done, With my hands handled or on my feet gone.

Verse 16: Vessel

The vessel of vinegar and of gall,
Lord, keep me from sins, them all
That to the soul be venom,
That I be not poisoned therein.

Verse 17: Vinegar and Gall

When you thirsted sorely with (it) all,
They gave you vinegar with bitter gall,
All that I have drunk in gluttony.
Before when I die Lord, forgive me.

Verse 18: Spear

Lord, the spear so sharp was/I ground,
That in thine heart made a wound,
It quenches the sin that I have wrought,
With all my heart full of evil thought.
And my stout pride also,
And my disobedience there too.

Verse 19: Ladder

The ladder set up for the occasion,
When you were dead to be taken down,
When that I am in sin,
Lord, let me not die therein.

Verse 20: Hammer

The hammer both stern and great,
That drove the nails through hand and foot.
Lord, be my succour in all my life,
If any man strike me with staff or knife.

Verse 21: Pliers

The tongs that drew the nails out,
Of feet and hands, all about.
And loosened your body from the tree,
Of my sins Lord, loosen me.

Verse 22: Spittle

The Jews that spit, Lord, in your face,
You suffered everything and gave them grace.
If I have guilt or any man (trespass against) me,
It be forgiven because of that pity.

Verse 23: Cross

The cross behind your backbone,
That you endured debts upon,
Lord, give me grace in my life,
To shrive me clean of sin.
And I to true repentance,
With an opportunity to perform my penance.

Verse 24: Sepulchre

The sepulchre wherein you were hid,
Your blessed body completely covered in blood,
Lord, grant me, before that I die,
Sorrow of heart, with tears of eye,
Purely cleansed by your mercy,
Before that I hasten into my grave,
So that I may at Judgement Day

To that judgement come without terror,
And approach to bliss in company,
There where men shall never die,
But dwell in bliss with that Lord bright,
Where it is always day but never night,
And last it shall without end,
Jesus Christ us thither send.

Printed in Great Britain
by Amazon

49676592R00128